CANYON COUNTRY

CANYON COUNTRY

PHOTOGRAPHY BY DEWITT JONES
TEXT BY STEPHEN TRIMBLE

GRAPHIC ARTS CENTER PUBLISHING COMPANY • PORTLAND, OREGON

International Standard Book Number 0-932575-07-2
Library of Congress Catalog Number 86-080097
Copyright © MCMLXXXVI by Graphic Arts Center Publishing Company
P.O. Box 10306 • Portland, Oregon 97210 • (503) 226-2402
Editor-in-Chief • Douglas A. Pfeiffer
Designer • Robert Reynolds
Cartographer • Thomas Patterson
Captions • Kathy Stevens
Typographer • Paul O. Giesey/Adcrafters
Printer • Graphic Arts Center
Bindery • Lincoln & Allen
Printed in the United States of America

To my daughter, DeAnna.
    Dewitt Jones

Frontispiece:
Twin symbols of the
Canyon Country, red rock
and desert sands form a
geologic circle of creation
and decay at Monument
Valley. The valley lies at
the geographic center of
the Colorado Plateau,
which covers 130,000
square miles of Utah,
Arizona, New Mexico,
and Colorado.

CANYON COUNTRY

National Parks (N.P.) and Monuments (N.M.)
National Recreation Areas (N.R.A.)
Indian Reservations (I.R.)
—— Major Highways

0   20   40   60 Miles
0 20 40 60 80 100 Kilometers

—N—

Great Salt Lake

Salt Lake City

FLAMING GORGE N.R.A.

UINTA × MOUNTAINS
Kings Peak 13528

Flaming Gorge Reservoir

DINOSAUR N.M.

Craig

Steamboat Springs

Vernal

Dinosaur

Duchesne
UINTAH AND OURAY I.R.

Yampa River

COLORADO UTAH

White River

Rangely

Meeker

Trappers Peak 11990 ×

THE FLAT TOPS

Price

Duchesne River

San Rafael River

GREEN RIVER

UINTAH AND OURAY I.R.

BOOK CLIFFS

ROAN PLATEAU

Rifle

RIVER

Glenwood Springs

COLORADO

Fillmore

Salina

Sevier River

WASATCH PLATEAU

Green River

Grand Junction

GRAND MESA

Leon Peak 11234 ×

Snowmass Peak 14092 ×

Richfield

ARCHES N.P.

COLORADO N.M.

Delta

GREAT BASIN

Sevier Lake

12173 × Delano Peak

Goblin Valley ×

Muddy Creek

Dead Horse Point ×

Mt Tomasaki 12271 ×

LA SAL MTS

UNCOMPAHGRE PLATEAU

BLACK CANYON OF THE GUNNISON N.M.

Montrose

Blue Mesa Lake

Beaver

Loa

CAPITOL REEF N.P.

Fremont River

Hanksville

Dirty Devil River

Moab

CANYONLANDS N.P.

Gunnison River

Dolores River

San Miguel River

Ouray

SAN JUAN

Panguitch

Brian Head × 11315

Boulder

Waterpocket Fold

HENRY MTS

ABAJO MTS 11019 ×

Monticello

Mt Wilson 14246 ×

MOUNTAINS

Cedar City

CEDAR BREAKS N.M.

AQUARIUS PLATEAU

Escalante

Escalante River

NATURAL BRIDGES N.M.

Blanding

Stoner

Windom Peak 14087 ×

Tropic

BRYCE CANYON N.P.

GLEN CANYON N.R.A.

Muley Point ×

Valley of the Gods ×

Montezuma Cr.

HOVENWEEP N.M.

Cortez

MESA VERDE N.P.

Durango

Pagosa Springs

ZION N.P.

Orderville

Paria River

Bluff

Goosenecks ×

San Juan

UTE MT. I.R.

S. UTE I.R.

St. George

Springdale

Kanab

Coral Pink Sand Dunes ×

UTAH
ARIZONA

Virgin River

MONUMENT VALLEY

COLORADO NEW MEXICO

Animas River

Navajo Lake

KAIBAB I.R.

PIPE SPRING N.M.

Kanab Creek

LAKE POWELL

RAINBOW BRIDGE N.M.

Page

Shiprock

AZTEC N.M.

JICARILLA APACHE I.R.

Jacob Lake

Chinle Wash

CARRIZO MTS

Ship Rock 7178 ×

Farmington

KAIBAB PLATEAU

NAVAJO N.M.

Kayenta

Lake Mead

COLORADO RIVER

North Rim

GRAND CANYON N.P.

Moenkopi

NAVAJO INDIAN RESERVATION

BLACK MESA

CHUSKA MOUNTAINS

CANYON DE CHELLY N.M.

Chinle

CHACO CANYON N.M.

Cuba

HUALAPAI I.R.

HAVASUPAI I.R.

Grand Canyon

COCONINO PLATEAU

Cameron

HOPI INDIAN RESERVATION

Polacca

NEW MEXICO ARIZONA

WUPATKI N.M.

Gallup

VOICES FROM THE SIX DIRECTIONS

The sun rises. Navajo people pray to the white dawn, to Grandfather Talking God. They thank the Holy People for life, for placing them in this land bounded by sacred mountains, this land of rivers and deserts and canyons. They offer a pinch of sacred cornmeal to each of the six directions: to the east, to the south, to the west, and to the north; to that point in the heavens most distant above, the zenith; and to the point in the earth most distant below, the nadir.

From these six directions they hear the voices of their Holy People, the land, the plants, and the animals. The voices tell the stories of this place called Canyon Country.

To learn the stories of Canyon Country, I traveled to each of the six directions. I listened to the land and I listened to its people.

The voices of the Canyon Country speak to us all. They come first at dawn, from the east.

FROM THE EAST

The glitter of stars in a blue-black sky dims. The palest of daylight begins to color the rim of rock below Delicate Arch. At first the rock is tan and shadowy, but slowly, softly, long after first light, the sun meets the horizon and brushes the stone landscape with a wash of orange-red.

The arch, a bold strut of sandstone, breaks the sky in two. Beyond the Colorado River, the highest peaks in Canyon Country — the La Sal Mountains, snow-capped well into summer — rise toward the flaring sun. Here in Arches National Park, in southeastern Utah, this single view captures the essences of the Canyon Country: red rock, river, island mountain, and the squared-off angles of mesas and plateaus everywhere between.

This is the Colorado Plateau. It begins where the Colorado River spills out of the Rocky Mountains in western Colorado and ends where the river leaves the Grand Canyon and enters the Mojave Desert in western Arizona. Between these points, the Colorado and its network of tributaries carve through 130,000 square miles of flat-lying rocks in the Four Corners states of Colorado, New Mexico, Utah, and Arizona.

Open basins, tabletop mesas, and arid badlands contribute to this plateau landscape. Green forests and blue mountains provide counterpoint and respite from the ocean of red rock. But at the heart of the Colorado Plateau are the canyons — carved deep by the Colorado, the Green, and the San Juan rivers and smaller tributaries like the Gunnison, Fremont, and Paria — and the great amphitheaters and gorges of Bryce and Zion, etched into the High Plateaus marking the region's western boundary.

A veil of water from Weeping Rock in Zion National Park lightly shields a view of the Great White Throne. Zion owes its lushness to the Virgin River, which bisects it, and to the porous Navajo Sandstone, which forms most of its great monoliths.

Canyon Country begins with the greatest of its rivers, the Colorado, flowing from Rocky Mountain National Park to the east. Confluences punctuate the course of the big river as it moves south and west across Canyon Country. It meets first with the Gunnison River at Grand Junction, Colorado. "Grand" refers to the old name for this upper stretch of the Colorado, which joins the Green River in Utah. Not until 1921 did the Colorado State Legislature secure the right to call the whole river stretching from the mountains to the sea by one name.

The Gunnison River first leaves the Rocky Mountains southeast of Grand Junction, near Montrose. Here it has carved a gorge through dark and ancient Precambrian gneiss. The Painted Wall, tapestried by light-colored volcanic dikes, rises 2,300 feet above the river in shadowed Black Canyon. The Gunnison ground through the resistant gneiss because it had no alternative: checked by growing volcanic mountains both to the north and south, the river cut down through the tough rock more than two thousand feet. Tributaries could not keep pace, so the Black Canyon today is both deep and narrow, measuring only 1,300 feet from rim to rim at the Narrows.

The Colorado flows on past its confluence with the Gunnison and passes around the north end of the Uncompahgre Plateau. Here, small red-rock canyons slice through the tip of the Uncompahgre. Colorado National Monument protects these canyons primarily because of the single-minded efforts of "crazy" John Otto, "the hermit of Monument Canyon."

Otto came to the cliffs above the green fields and orchards of Grand Valley in 1907 and quickly became obsessed with the place. He lived among the sandstone monoliths and canyons for thirty years, building trails and promoting in a stream of letters to editors and politicians what he called, "the highest class Park Project in all Creation."

On the Fourth of July, 1910, he climbed 530-foot-tall Independence Monument and unfurled an American flag from its summit. A year later, he was married at its base, but his wife left after just two months, explaining: "I could not live with a man to whom even a cabin was an encumbrance. He wanted to live in tents or without tents, outdoors." That year, Otto may have lost his new wife, but his primary obsession meshed with the interests of local boosters and legislators, and the land he loved became a national monument, protected by law.

Otto had endless enthusiasm for his home. He felt sure that the Grand Canyon would have to "split honors with Colorado National Monument from now on." Describing the canyons as "the heart of the world," he called the area surrounding them "without doubt the most interesting part of the earth's crust that's known." Not a man to back off from superlatives, he once wrote:

It's in Colorado where one finds: the sunniest of sunshine, the bluest of sky, the grandest of scenery, the coolest of mountains, the prettiest of soil, the choicest of fruit, the sweetest of melons, the finest of gardens, the truest of homes, the gayest of youngsters, the cutest and the sweetest of faces, and the HAPPIEST OF PEOPLE.

7

As the monument's first custodian, Otto was responsible for building the "Trail of the Serpent...so people could drive where only the birds could fly before." He introduced buffalo into the canyons by asking everybody in town to donate their buffalo nickels to pay for a small herd, and he campaigned against the annual decimation of "the pretty little Christmas trees."

Otto was not the first, or the last, of the solitaries whose preference for places over people helped shape the future of Canyon Country. Down the Colorado from Otto's haunts, near Moab, Utah, Hungarian immigrant Alexander Ringhoffer prospected the slickrock sculpture garden known today as Klondike Bluffs in 1922. He found no minerals, but the rocky scenery so impressed him that he contacted the Denver and Rio Grande Railroad about developing the area for tourists. His ideas eventually led to Arches' designation as a national monument in 1929 and as a national park in 1971.

Freestanding arcs of stone are called natural bridges if they span a watercourse, arches if they do not. Arches can form on the edges of cliffs, where a pothole grinds through, or when an alcove in a fin deepens, piercing the wall, but the reason for the remarkable concentration of natural stone spans at Arches National Park is more complicated.

Uplift during the last 10 million years has raised the great island of flat rocks that forms the Colorado Plateau to an average elevation of five thousand feet above sea level with some plateaus and island mountain ranges reaching twice that height, despite erosion. Most of the Canyon Country remained unbroken during uplift. But in places, the rocks bent and fractured along lines of weakness. Sharp breaks or faults raised plateaus and dropped valleys. Bends created S-shaped monoclines, larger upwarps, or dome-shaped anticlines. Sometimes, rocks simply shattered in parallel cracks and joint systems.

Such joints laced Arches' Entrada Sandstone. Salt flowing deep underground and doming up the sandstone layers above also made joints. Uplift and erosion continued, layer after layer washed away, and when groundwater reached and dissolved the salt, the domed layers above collapsed, widening and further fracturing the joints. Rain and winter ice accentuated the cracks, leaving fins of sandstone standing high between them. Holes eroded through the fins. Small windows grew into arches.

Salt, three thousand feet of it, deposited in a drying inland sea 300 million years ago, underlies most of southeastern Utah. It has helped form erosional fantasies south of Arches as well, in Canyonlands National Park.

Canyonlands was Bates Wilson's park. For fifteen years he spent his days off from his job as superintendent of Arches exploring the rough country to the south and promoting its importance to all who would listen. He became a master of both public relations and Dutch-oven camp cooking — sometimes performing the two at once when entertaining politicians in the backcountry. When he won over Stewart Udall, Secretary of the Interior under President John F. Kennedy, events moved quickly and Canyonlands became a national park in 1964.

As superintendent of both Arches and Canyonlands, Bates protected huge pieces of Canyon Country. He also protected the parks' uninitiated visitors. In the early days at Arches, Bates rescued tourists stranded when flash floods boomed down Courthouse Wash after late summer storms. He would build a fire and cheer his guests with stories, food, and hot coffee until the wash dried enough for them to move on.

Bates repeatedly rejected official plans for developing Squaw Flat Campground in Canyonlands; he did not want a rock touched. Finally, exasperated planners told him to do it himself, and Bates proceeded to do just that, carefully laying out campsites between junipers and fins. Today the campground is one of the most soothing in Canyon Country.

Slim Mabery worked for Bates Wilson in the early 1960s; in turn, Edward Abbey worked for Slim while rangering at Arches and working on *Desert Solitaire,* the book that introduced a generation to the Canyon Country wilderness. Slim first saw the Moab Valley in May of 1947. Pear trees were in blossom and fresh snow gleamed on the La Sal Mountains beyond the little green village nestled in the red rocks. Slim thought it was the prettiest sight he had ever seen. Since then, he has worked as ranger and jeep-tour guide in the canyonland country around Moab and has become something of a local legend.

Slim recalls with amusement the hearings for the proposed Canyonlands National Park:

The miners had been in there and they couldn't find a thing; the cattle would starve to death, and they did have to haul water. Their check dams wouldn't last a season — a flash flood would come along and take them out. They all decided it wasn't worth a dadgone thing for anything, and they might as well give it back to the Indians. Then it was proposed as a national park, and suddenly it became really rich in mineral deposits, good hunting grounds, good livestock grazing.

Canyonlands' high mesas look out over the canyons of the Colorado and Green rivers, joined deep in the stone labyrinth below Dead Horse and Grand View points. Halfway down lie the benchlands, encircled north of the confluence by the hundred-mile-long White Rim jeep road. On the west side of the confluence is The Maze; on the east, The Needles.

Beneath The Needles, the entire salt bed deep within the Paradox Formation is moving toward the Colorado River, tugging at surface rocks. The overlying layers break under the stress and form the straight-sided valleys called The Grabens. Slim has seen check dams for stock tanks breached and roads made impassable by fresh earth movement between jeep trips to the area.

Deep winter snow cloaks the pinnacles and spires, obelisks and hoodoos of Bryce Canyon, more accurately called an amphitheater than a canyon. With only 36,010 acres, Bryce is the smallest of the seven national parks in the Canyon Country. Its average elevation is eight thousand feet.

The array of fins in Canyonlands and Arches creates landscapes of sandstone hoodoos and hobgoblins, winding joints and slots, whose names sum up their whimsical, elaborate architecture: The Maze, Lost Canyon, Devil's Garden, the Fiery Furnace, the Windows, the Doll House, Courthouse Towers.

Aridity keeps the rocky tablelands free of dense vegetation and soil. Juniper and piñon pine survive among the rocks; grasses and desert shrubs—blackbrush and saltbush—grow in the sandy swales between. The rivers, fed by snowmelt in the distant Rockies, and ephemeral streams running only in flood sweep erosional debris toward the sea, leaving the rock bare and clean, clearing the valleys and canyons of rubble. Stone unadorned by soil molds the Canyon Country, shaping the views and the lives of those who come here.

FROM THE SOUTH

Indian voices come from the south—Navajo and Pueblo voices and the ancient voices of the Anasazi, ancestors of the Pueblo people. On Colorado's Mesa Verde, the Anasazi voices ring pure. Few other people have lived there. Along the San Juan River, northern border of Navajo Country, and in the small canyons farther south—the Tsegi, Canyon de Chelly, and Chaco Canyon—the three voices mingle. In Monument Valley, they murmur in the wind that blows around red mesas and buttes.

The Colorado Plateau extends farther south, but badlands and sweeping desert grassland replace canyons as the defining landscapes. Most streams are not big enough to carve deep. Canyons like Chaco lie small and isolated in a huge plateau under an even bigger sky. Canyon de Chelly hides within the flanks of the Chuska Mountains. It is Monument Valley with its isolated mesas that symbolizes the southern Canyon Country.

Once, the monuments-to-be were connected within a broad plateau. As stormwater ran down through the joints between blocks, slots widened, and mesas became detached from the ends of plateaus. Wider than they are high, mesas eroded to buttes, which are higher than wide, and then to monuments—narrow spires fated to topple. The spaces between the monuments used to be rock. Now they are canyons—wide ones.

From a distance, Monument Valley looks horizontal. The mesas stand in rows, separating earth and sky. But up close, at the base of the Totem Pole or the Mittens, the valley turns vertical, the walls of the mesas as sheer as any canyon.

It is hard to picture Monument Valley without a flock of sheep and a scattering of Navajo hogans, round houses facing east to the dawn. But despite that familiar image, this has been Navajo Country for little more than a century.

Evening primrose adorns the land around Capitol Reef National Park, some of the last territory explored in the continental United States. The nearly impassable barrier of rock that shapes most of the park reminded frustrated pioneers of an ocean reef.

For the Hopi it is not Navajo Country at all. Hopi people lived in northern Arizona for hundreds, if not thousands, of years before the Navajo came. The Hopi, pueblo-dwellers like the Anasazi before them, maintain an intimate and intense relationship with the land around their villages. The Navajo, who have surrounded them, call themselves Diné, The People.

Today, Diné Bikéyah, Navajo Country, stretches across the southern third of Canyon Country. The Navajo Reservation itself spans twenty-five thousand square miles, nearly one-fifth of the entire Colorado Plateau. The sacred mountains tie Navajo land together, rising hazy blue or snowy white above dun and tan and rust-colored mesas.

Here, according to Navajo legend, Father Sky meets Mother Earth; here the two match in scale. Steven Darden, a young Navajo who has served on the Flagstaff, Arizona, City Council, explains it like this:

Here is Father Sky, pressing right there, united with the earth. The fog and the dew and the rain, the clouds, they all sit there on the earth. There is that union, Mother Earth and Father Sky. They are complementary; they generate life. That's the Navajo way.

Navajos and Apaches—together, the Apacheans—have their nearest relations far to the north in Canada and Alaska. Sometime before 1600, the Apacheans moved south, toward Canyon Country. Most Apacheans were nomads, but one group incorporated more of the Pueblo lifeway, started farming, and became the people we call the Navajo.

In 1539, another culture entered the Southwest. The Spanish brought the Indian people difficulty and death, but they also brought the horse, and the Apacheans became the first mounted Indians north of Mexico. When Pueblo people sought refuge with the Navajo after their rebellion against the Spanish in 1680, Pueblo weavers added to what Spider Woman had taught the Navajo. The result has been remarkable rugs with noble names like Two Grey Hills, Wide Ruins, Tees Nos Pas, and Ganado.

Two hundred years of alternating peace and warfare between Navajo raiders and Spanish, Mexican, and American settlers followed the Pueblo Rebellion. Then, in 1863, the United States Army delivered the final, harsh blow to Navajo freedom. In that last campaign, Kit Carson penetrated the heartland of Navajo Country, Canyon de Chelly, home of Anasazi ruins and Navajo gods. He killed few Navajo compared to the Spanish, but he destroyed the crops and herds of the Diné at the beginning of winter, and the starving Navajo surrendered.

Fully half the tribe—more than eight thousand people—spent the next four years in disastrous captivity at Fort Sumner in eastern New Mexico. The rest escaped westward, deeper into the canyons. Finally, in 1868, the exiled Navajo returned home and, with their kin who had remained behind, began to build the modern Navajo nation.

Non-Indian ways penetrated Navajo Country with the trading posts. Among the traders were the Wetherill family from Mancos, Colorado, who discovered the big cliff dwellings at Mesa

Verde in the 1880s and ran trading posts around Chaco Canyon, New Mexico. In 1906, John Wetherill, following in the footsteps of Hoskininni, the Navajo leader who evaded Kit Carson, moved his family to Oljato, Utah. Tucked behind a red mesa around the corner from Monument Valley, the Wetherills were the first white settlers in isolated country which traditionally had been Paiute. Wetherill and his wife, Louisa, traded with the Navajo and Paiute, lived with them, and became their guides in dealing with the outside world. In return, the Indians guided Wetherill to Rainbow Bridge, to the great cliff dwellings of Betatakin and Keet Seel, and to a hundred other canyons.

After World War II, Ed Smith moved to Oljato with his new bride, Chin Carson. Ed first came to Canyon Country riding for the Indian Motorcycle Company in a cross-country race in the 1930s. He liked what he saw and, after cowpunching all over the Four Corners, he settled in Oljato. He has been there ever since, grumbling about it with a twinkle in his eye. He describes how the trading business worked until, "Everything turned to cash all the way around."

> You bought the groceries on credit. You traded the groceries for rugs, for sheep, for anything. If a guy killed a coyote, he'd bring the coyote skin in to you. You'd say, well I wonder how the hell much I can get for this. . . . Then you sent that back to where you bought the groceries; they figured the valuation and credited your account. It was just a big guessing game, but it was kind of fun.

> You didn't make any money. If you didn't like living there you were wasting your time. . . .

Ed saw the changes that came to the Navajo Reservation after World War II, when for the first time many of the *Diné* saw the outside world. He laments watching the Navajo "meet the same stumbling blocks that the white man met." He talks bitterly about administrative boondoggles, nonsensical regulations, and "big-shot" politicians, some federal, some tribal.

But he lists his religion as Old Navajo when he checks into a hospital, and when he talks, he interrupts his cynicism with a heartfelt "Thank God for the Navajo."

* * *

Summer solstice. Across the mesas and cliffs of Canyon Country, shafts of light illuminate ancient drawings carved into stone. At Chaco Canyon, New Mexico, high on the flanks of a butte called Fajada, a dagger of light appears at noon. Hovering above a spiral petroglyph, the light moves downward, passing through the center of the spiral.

These sun calendars mark solstice and equinox. They are hundreds of years old. We call the people who made them Anasazi — the prehistoric Pueblo people.

People lived in the canyons for at least ten thousand years before becoming farmers. By about 700 A.D., many had settled down in villages near their cornfields and had homesteaded the nooks and crannies of Canyon Country. Fremont people lived in the north, from Capitol Reef to Dinosaur; Anasazi lived in the south, in Four Corners country.

For many centuries Anasazi planted their crops when their solar calendars said the time was right. Their voices rang out in the canyons, alive with the rhythm of ceremonies attuned to germination, cultivation, and harvest. Then the canyon dwellers moved on, restless, their fields depleted.

The Anasazi people developed their most sophisticated culture between 900 and 1150 A.D. at Chaco Canyon, where the great pueblos stood four and five stories high, with hundreds of rooms surrounding large ceremonial structures called great kivas. They had abundant luxuries: inlaid turquoise jewelry, copper bells, macaws kept for feathers. Building water-control systems, they diverted runoff from summer storms to their terraced fields. But by the late 1200s, they had abandoned Chaco.

Mesa Verde and the northern San Juan River country saw a second flowering of Anasazi culture. But unlike Chaco, this area never showed formal community organization; it was simply a complex of neighboring pueblos. Even the spectacular cliff dwellings of the 1200s, such as Cliff Palace, the 217-room centerpiece of Mesa Verde National Park, may have been backwaters of the San Juan Anasazi culture. Pueblos below the mesa, in the valleys around Cortez, Colorado, were larger and possessed a spectacular number of kivas.

The great cliff houses of Betatakin and Keet Seel in the Tsegi canyons of Arizona's Navajo National Monument also developed late in the 1200s. Their people, the Kayenta Anasazi, lived in these enormous alcoves of golden Navajo Sandstone for only a short time. Leaving Mesa Verde and the San Juan drainage — including the Tsegi — by 1300, the Anasazi had abandoned many other traditional homelands by 1450.

Environmental disasters may have forced some to move, but many may have chosen to emigrate, their leave-taking announced by a clan leader when he felt it was time to embark on prophesied migrations. Over decades and centuries, whole populations shifted to Hopi, Zuñi, and Acoma pueblos and new homes along the Rio Grande.

Today, the ruined pueblos at Chaco Canyon stand as a monument to the accomplishments of Anasazi culture. Pueblo Bonito and a handful of other "great houses" lie within Chaco Canyon itself; dozens of outlying villages extend to the limits of the San Juan Basin like the spokes of an irregular wheel. Elsewhere, remnants of great pueblo civilizations are often concealed by vegetation, inundated by silt, or disguised by modern civilization. But at Chaco, arid climate has preserved the ruins. Archeologist Michael Marshall calls the area "one big mummy."

Salt from a vanished sea underlies the red-rock landscape of Arches National Park. Over millions of years, the movement of the salt and regional uplift created parallel fractures in the overlying rock. These fractures eroded, fins of rock appeared between them, and recesses in the fins weathered into arches.

Marshall and colleague John Stein describe Chaco as a "Meca-like" place of pilgrimage, the center of a sacred landscape marked by mountains, hills, water sources, dry lake beds — all integrated with mythological history. Marshal hypothesizes that each great pueblo represents an outlying district of people who came here for public ceremonies: "Chaco didn't create the outlying villages; they created Chaco."

If Chaco was the center of the twelfth-century Anasazi world, Pueblo Alto was its sentinel and gateway. The ruin sits on the north rim above the canyon, a few walls protruding from the earth. At least five prehistoric roads, barely visible now, converge at this site, although the Anasazi had no wheeled vehicles. What they used the roads for remains unknown.

In autumn, the world falls away northward from Pueblo Alto in a mosaic of earth-tones: the pale straw of ricegrass and galleta grass, brown-green sagebrush on the uplands, green and gold rabbitbrush along the banks of the dry riverbeds. The Great North Road is a subtle grassy path between darker rows of winter saltbush. The wind kicks up in Escavada Wash, a river of sand and dust, generating backlit clouds of light.

At dusk, the great kiva of Casa Rinconada, roofless, is filled with ancient echoes, with the sounds of a hundred Anasazi chanters and drummers. Snarled tumbleweeds fill each of the masonry postholes. The moon is up in the east, three days short of full. Rinconada's walls enclose an elegant ellipse of colored sky, turquoise on the eastern horizon, shading through light lavender to transparent violet at the zenith.

The moon arcs through this curve of sky. The kiva is an observatory, a receptacle for solstice sunbeams. The canyon is a compass, laid out east-west, the sun track's annual shift across the sky a major event, linked to what architects call sacred geometry. Lookout posts mark promontories; shrines and tower kivas punctuate the straight lines of prehistoric roads.

John Stein says: "We don't yet know what the prehistoric roads were used for. But there is no other Chaco Canyon in the Anasazi world. All roads lead to Chaco."

FROM THE WEST

Voices from the western Canyon Country are Mormon voices: "In southern Utah," says rancher Met Johnson, "I feel culturally enriched. Here I feel like I have a heritage of two hundred years. If I go someplace else, I feel like I'm just barely a day old."

Met Johnson might exaggerate Mormon residency in southern Utah by a few years, but he is right about the heritage of this place. Southern Utah is slickrock country and Mormon country.

The 730-mile-long Green River, which begins in west-central Wyoming, winds its way through the center of Dinosaur National Monument before converging with the Colorado River. Dinosaur lies in both northeastern Utah and northwestern Colorado and marks the beginning of the Colorado Plateau.

The Mormons entered this country from the west. It begins abruptly, at Zion, the ultimate slickrock canyon. The vertical cliffs and temples above the canyon, the lunar knobs and massive buttes around Checkerboard Mesa — these are mountains more than mesas, mountains of sandstone carved from what feels like a single block of earth.

The most impressive of these mountains is the symbol of Zion National Park, the Great White Throne. When it rains, mists lower and swirl around the monolith, parting to expose polished white stone, but never revealing the summit. The Throne does not appear to end but goes on, up and up into the silver mist.

The colors of desert varnish staining the rocks deepen when wet. Red turns to purple; iron-rich layers capping hoodoos become still-richer black. The mist blocks the glare of Canyon Country sun, revealing images often missed in the heat: a severed juniper root, corkscrewed by slow growth, on clean, wind-swept sand; a single prickly pear, furry with spines, sprouting from naked, banded sandstone.

Everything in Zion matches the grand scale of the Great White Throne. Instead of the more humble piñon and juniper of lesser canyons, full-sized pine and fir grown on the ledges. The Virgin River is no diminutive ephemeral stream but a permanent watercourse spilling down from the eleven thousand-foot summit of the Markagunt Plateau.

The Virgin carves through Navajo Sandstone. In the Narrows, it runs at its steepest gradient—130 feet per mile—and in flood it slices through the rock like a ripsaw. Only sixteen feet of water and slippery cobbles separate the cool, thousand-foot-tall walls of stone, the fine-grained sandstone strong enough to rise the full height of the canyon without collapsing.

The cliffs retreat from the Virgin River when it runs into softer rocks. It undercuts the great walls of Navajo Sandstone, and enormous sheets of rock peel off and crash to the valley floor. The canyon widens; the river washes the rubble downstream. Zion's resulting U-shaped canyon looks deceptively glacial, Yosemite-like, especially after a snowstorm.

Zion Canyon is carved out of one of the High Plateaus of western Utah, a barricade standing over eleven thousand feet high. Flat-topped and capped with resistant lava, they support forests and meadows liberally watered with summer rain and winter snow. Their eastern flanks drop toward lower country undisturbed by faults and toward huge expanses of sandstone, where rivers fed by the plateaus have created a bewildering latticework of canyons.

The deepest canyons exist where rivers cleave high plateaus: Zion Canyon in the Markagunt Plateau, the Paria River Narrows in the Paria Plateau, and the Grand Canyon of the Colorado within the Kaibab Plateau. Between the plateaus and the Colorado in Glen Canyon, tributary streams wind through deserts of naked stone and cut through the occasional upwarp among flat-lying rocks. The Escalante, Hall's Creek, the Fremont and Dirty Devil, the San Rafael — these streams dissect huge expanses of sandstone into a fretwork of slots, rims, domes, and reefs.

A half century ago, a young, romantic wanderer named Everett Ruess came to slickrock country with his burros to explore "southward to the Colorado, where no one lives." Nobody knows what happened to the twenty-one-year-old Ruess; he vanished in the canyons in 1934. Before his disappearance, he sent a last letter to his brother. He was writing from south of Escalante, "on what seems like the rim of the world":

I prefer the saddle to the streetcar and star-sprinkled sky to a roof, the obscure and difficult trail, leading into the unknown, to any paved highway, and the deep peace of the wild to the discontent bred by cities. Do you blame me then for staying here, where I feel that I belong and am one with the world around me?

These canyons still offer the same peaceful isolation, for they were never settled and barely used, even by the Mormons. Today, Lake Powell drowns their lower reaches, but the remaining canyons—still places "where no one lives"—look much as they did to Everett Ruess or even to the pioneering wagons of the Hole-in-the-Rock colonists, who struggled across southern Utah in 1880 in the name of God and their prophet.

Brigham Young brought his flock to Salt Lake City in 1847 and within ten years established the Church of Jesus Christ of Latter-day Saints in their new state of Deseret. The Mormons came to this wilderness to escape persecution, and the Church remained single-minded about making their domain permanent. They colonized southward along the base of the Colorado Plateau to St. George and what they called "Dixie"—a southern outpost where they grew cotton, made wine, and ministered to Paiute Indians. Then they turned east, looking for new land.

The 1860s were difficult, as the Mormon frontier jarred hard against the Navajo moving north to escape the U.S. Army. By 1870, of the nearly 3 million acres of Kane County around Kanab, 1,244 had been "improved," and county authorities guessed that only twenty acres of potential agricultural land remained undeveloped. By 1876, tiny Mormon towns, their wide streets lined with shade trees and rock houses, had begun to spread. Cannonville, Henrieville, and, later, Tropic were established in the Paria Amphitheater below Bryce Canyon. Escalante and Boulder took root on the upper reaches of the Escalante River. Other villagers pushed down the Fremont River, founding Loa, Bicknell, and Torrey in the 1870s, and reached the limits of irrigable land at Hanksville in 1880. Beyond lay canyons without even a twenty-acre chance for farming.

To reach Hanksville, the villagers had to pass through Capitol Reef, which they named for the barrier of sandstone that felt as absolute as an ocean reef. Passage here was not over or past the reef, but *through* it in the deep narrows of Capitol Gorge. Today's highway curves easily with the Fremont River through Capitol Reef National Park, but this route was not opened until 1962, and the river had to be rechanneled to accomplish it.

The reef forms the steepest face of the Waterpocket Fold, a monocline that stretches south for almost one hundred miles to the Colorado River. Its Navajo Sandstone summit contains the symmetrical domes and the dependable waterpockets that give the place its alternate names.

The family of a park ranger recently refused to visit him at Capitol Reef because it was "too dark." The lack of reassuring streetlights in the old Mormon village of Fruita, now park headquarters, evidently frightened them, but of all the words to apply to Capitol Reef, "dark" fits least.

From the top of the fold, light fills the sky, bounces from the rocks, and penetrates into the deepest of side canyons, where it reflects between the walls so many times it seems to acquire the density and color of well-aged bourbon. Above the Burr Trail (the only road across the southern part of the park), or at Muley Twist Overlook, the jagged remnants of the reef lead away in cliffs likened to whalebacks and shark teeth. Short side canyons lead out to Hall's Creek, which parallels the fold along its lower half, between the cliffs of Capitol Reef and the austere Mancos Shale facade of Tarantula Mesa to the east.

What is not rock is light. The moon illuminates the country almost as brightly as the sun. Here you dwell in an expanse of stone and light that takes in most of southern Utah, from the High Plateaus in the west, out past the Henry Mountains, to Monument Valley and Canyonlands in the east. Everywhere is slickrock—slickrock and light.

* * *

In some places in the West, the Frontier ended in 1880. But not in southern Utah. The Church of Latter-day Saints had not yet pushed past the Colorado to the San Juan, and despite Brigham Young's death in 1877, colonization remained a divine imperative. The call went out and wagons gathered south of Escalante. An amphitheater near the rendezvous point at Forty Mile Spring proved a fine place for fiddles and has been called Dance Hall Rock ever since.

Once the trip started, however, there was no time for dancing. Silas Smith and Platte Lyman led more than two hundred and fifty people through six months of heroic labor in a "short cut" across incredibly difficult terrain to found Bluff on the San Juan River. To ford the Colorado, they blasted a road—the Hole-in-the-Rock—into Glen Canyon. The task took six weeks, the time they had allotted for the entire trip. Beyond the river, they built dugways, hauled wagons through sand, and skidded and slogged through the muck of snow-drenched clay.

They had aimed for Montezuma Creek, but when they reached the first acceptable bottomlands on the San Juan River in April, 1880, just eighteen miles from their original goal, they ground to a halt. Enough was enough. Cottonwood Wash might

A native of Asia and southeast Europe, tamarisk was brought west for use as an ornamental early in the twentieth century. Proliferating along Canyon Country waterways, it consumes precious water and can displace native plants.

wash away their fields, the San Juan might flood their homes, but they would go no further. Their mission was completed.

How much has it all changed? The year 1880 now lies more than a century behind us, but that century has brought less change to southern Utah than to most places.

Met Johnson lives half the year on a thirteen thousand-acre ranch up the East Fork of the Sevier River, north of Bryce, and spends the other half along a curve of asphalt in a Cedar City subdivision. About the ranch he says, "There's no question that this is still the frontier. We're brand new in this area really."

Wilderness still exists here — in national parks, in empty public lands, and on the rangelands where ranchers make their living. Met Johnson says:

I like to work hard and be alone and be out—I mean really out. I think it cleanses your mind and your attitude and your soul. I think it cleanses your ambition. It's like taking a real good X-ray of yourself and damn sure having it honest.

You can't hardly even be with anybody because the only thing you can take to that experience is yourself. When your soul touches whatever it touches, it cannot be limited. You can't have a boundary of how long you'll stay or how cold you'll feel or how hot you'll feel. If you try to control any of the elements of that environment, that exposure, then you interrupt the message.

How in hell are you ever going to tell anybody about it? I really don't care to tell anybody about it. I hope they all go find it, but I hope they don't go to find it on the same rock I'm sitting on!

FROM THE NORTH

From the north flows the Green River. It carves off the eastern end of the Uinta Mountains at Dinosaur National Monument, rolls peaceably through the Uinta Basin, and then enters the Tavaputs Plateau, breaching the Book Cliffs at the town of Green River. Farther south, the Green runs into the canyonlands toward its confluence with the Colorado.

The river bubbles and froths and roils. Though the mountain men called it by the Crow Indian name *Seedskeedee*, in Utah the language the river speaks is Ute.

The Ute Nation once embraced the Colorado Rockies and eastern Utah from Salt Lake City to Denver, from Wyoming to New Mexico. "The Utes belong in the mountains," says Clifford Duncan, director of the tribal museum at Fort Duchesne, Utah, at the foot of the Uintas.

I could never live anywhere else. I identify myself with the mountains. To me, landscape is a compass, it helps to keep

me where I'm at. When I go to Kansas or Oklahoma, where there's no mountains, it's flat, there is nothing there to control you. But here I know where I am. All I have to do is look up at the mountains.

Utes like Clifford Duncan still look up to their mountains. But no mountains lie within their reservations, for in the late 1800s prospectors and cattlemen limited the Utes to the drier, less desirable canyons and plateaus. "Spiritually we consider the old original Ute nation as being ours still," says Duncan. "You can physically take it, but you can't take it away from a person's mind. There are still ties there — sacred spots, sacred plants, medicines that are still out there."

Both mountains and streams help to define the spirit of the Utes. Clifford explains why:

Water from here, streams coming from this mountain, will be different from that water that, say, is coming from Wyoming or the Plains or the Southwest. I am part of this water. If you give me another water, it changes the chemistry of my body, and I get sick. It changes the way I think, too. So that's why we say water is sacred to us. It gives life.

The life-giving water of the Green River, of the *Seedskeedee*, forms a major barrier to travel in the northern Canyon Country. Only two major crossings exist even today, near Vernal in the Uinta Basin and at Green River at the base of the Book Cliffs. North to south, enormous bands of precipitous canyons and plateaus alternate with easier country.

The northernmost canyons lie in Dinosaur National Monument, where the Yampa River joins the Green, and the augmented river hews its way through Split Mountain and out into the Uinta Basin. Where layers of rock have been upended and then eroded to hogbacks below Split Mountain, the Green River flows past the dinosaur quarry where Earl Douglass first chipped out seven *Brontosaurus* vertebrae in 1909.

These bones, about 150 million years old, were found in the Morrison Formation. Deposited midway into the reign of dinosaurs, in the Jurassic period, the Morrison Formation crops out in many places, but the Douglass quarry is one of the richest in fossils. Early dinosaur fossils are found in the Chinle and Kayenta formations in Arizona's Painted Desert and Navajo Country. Bones from the last of the giant reptiles come from the Fruitland-Kirtland formations in New Mexico's San Juan Basin.

Fifty million years after Chinle time, the dinosaurs had come to dominate the earth. Morrison dinosaurs ranged from graceful birdlike animals just four feet long that probably lived on lizards to the huge *Brontosaurus, Diplodocus, Stegosaurus,* and *Allosaurus.* (*Brontosaurus* and the fierce carnivore *Allosaurus* have been renamed *Apatosaurus* and *Antrodemus,* but the older names remain better known.) A few miles east of Dinosaur National Monument, new discoveries not yet fully studied have yielded the largest dinosaurs of all — "Supersaurus" and its allies. When walking the tropical Canyon Country world of the Jurassic period, they must have weighed more than a hundred tons, twenty times as heavy as a modern elephant.

Water, the master sculptor of the Canyon Country, slowly carves away at soft sandstone rock and creates a range of graceful forms and shapes. The fluted walls of a sandstone slot near Glen Canyon exhibit the work of an intermittent stream.

At the Douglass quarry, dinosaur carcasses had accumulated on a sandbar in a shallow Morrison river where they washed aground. The concentration of bones was astounding. Working through this tangle of skeletons from thirteen species of dinosaurs, Douglass shipped almost three hundred tons of fossils east to Pennsylvania's Carnegie Museum.

During fifteen years of work, Douglass saw the quarry achieve national monument status. He and his wife, Pearl, spent the first long winter huddled over their cookstove by night, reading aloud the reports of the early Canyon Country geologists, John Wesley Powell and his compatriots. Later, they built a house, settled in, and raised prize vegetables.

Today, Dinosaur National Monument includes the canyons of the Green and Yampa rivers. Neighboring Artesia, Colorado, has changed its name to Dinosaur and designated its streets with names like Stegosaurus Freeway and Brontosaurus Boulevard. At the quarry, excavation continues, but most bones remain in place in Dinosaur Ledge, enclosed by a visitor center.

Nearby, the Green River flows from the maw of Split Mountain, its waters reflecting great cliffs then looping away into the Uinta Basin, where the river slows. In summer, clouds of mosquitoes hum in the cottonwood groves along its banks. In autumn, the wind riffles a carpet of fallen cottonwood leaves on the night of a full moon, and the silver moonlight seems to flow across the ground. In winter, ground fog blankets gold-stubbled meadows, red willows, and leafless trees quiet in the mist.

Along this easy stretch of the river, the Spanish friars Domínguez and Escalante found a crossing in 1776, on their way west to search for an overland route from Santa Fe to the Pacific Coast. They were the first Europeans to explore deep into Canyon Country and although they did not reach California, they did return home safely, and the map of their travels influenced exploration for decades. Many others followed them through the Uinta Basin, for downstream the Green disappears into cliffs, winding its way through Desolation and Gray canyons.

Desolation is sunk five thousand·feet deep into the Tavaputs Plateau. The Tavaputs ends southward at the Book Cliffs, a barrier as imposing as the river itself. Eastward from Price, Utah, to Grand Junction, Colorado, they stand in what John Wesley Powell called "one of the most wonderful facades of the world... a land of desolation, dedicated forever to the geologist and the artist. ..." At the base of the Book Cliffs, the Green River enters Labyrinth and Stillwater canyons and merges with the Colorado deep "under the rim" in Canyonlands National Park.

* * *

These wild canyons did not suffer pioneers willingly. By the 1880s, the Frontier was fading fast, but frontier conflict continued as pioneers moved on to cattle-raising once they used up farmland. Cattlemen and sheepmen eyed the rare water holes and limited range with concern — and sometimes eyed each other over the sights of their rifles.

Small homesteaders battling with big absentee landholders had minimal respect for laws that did little to protect them. Soon, cattle-rustling became a viable profession. Its practitioners blazed a new trail across Canyon Country: the Outlaw Trail.

Outlaws who started rustling needed a hideout to consolidate their herd before moving it on for sale. They chose an isolated rim above the Green River near its confluence with the Colorado. Box canyons and narrow mesas surrounded them and protected the hideout from surprise approach from the east. Westward, the San Rafael Desert fell away to the Henry Mountains in fifty miles of red sand and delicate golden puffs of Indian ricegrass. Any rider could be seen approaching for miles.

The hideout had been known as Robber's Roost for more than fifteen years when Butch Cassidy and his partners rode in after the Castle Gate bank robbery in 1897.

Butch Cassidy was a robber and an outlaw but not a killer. His friends across much of the West judged him a good man, if one judges a man by his kindness, his generosity, and his integrity in dealing with his peers. Born into a solid Mormon family in Circleville, Utah, near Bryce, Butch started life as Robert Leroy Parker. He took to banditry largely because he was outraged over being framed for horse-stealing by big ranching interests. Once started, he said, it was hard to turn back.

Butch and other outlaws rode the Green River between Robber's Roost (above The Maze in Canyonlands) and Brown's Hole, Colorado (later Dinosaur National Monument). Local legend says they used a dugout in Capitol Reef's Grand Wash when they came through from the High Plateaus.

Butch knew every rancher along the way and attributed his success in evading capture to a single gift: "friends." As Jim McPherson, who homesteaded at Florence Creek Ranch in Desolation Canyon in 1890, once remarked, "The outlaws were generally a lot nicer folks than the posse chasing 'em."

In 1902, Butch and the Sundance Kid escaped to South America a whisper ahead of Pinkerton detectives. Long after rumor said he died in a shoot-out in South America in 1908, stories surfaced of Butch visiting his old friends in Utah and Wyoming. The stories proved true. The Sundance Kid died in Bolivia; his lady, Etta Place, lived out her life as the wife of a government official in Paraguay. But Butch Cassidy escaped to Spokane, Washington, to become William T. Phillips, a respectable businessman who died in 1937.

Pearl Baker helped track down much of this story, and she had reason to do so: she grew up at Robber's Roost Ranch, where her father, Joe Biddlecome, took over the the range in 1909 after the outlaws moved on. Pearl's opinions about ranching in these canyons are mixed with seventy-five years of memories and are

Muley Point Overlook on the eastern border of Glen Canyon National Recreation Area offers a panoramic view of Monument Valley to the south and the San Juan River more than one thousand feet below. The San Juan joins the Colorado at Lake Powell.

impassioned by a decade of running the Roost herd herself, in the 1930s. She says:

I resent that a dude from Boston — book-trained rather than range-trained—thinks he has as much right to this land as I do, when I build trails, dig out waterholes, move cattle around to protect the range, and treat it as a precious heritage and a trust. I resent the fact that all cattlemen are represented as greedy opportunists who rape the range to graze just one more cow. This was our country. We were the people who made the rules at the Roost.

But Pearl also believes: "There is something about this country that is deeper than just being here. There is a spiritual quality about it too, that is as deep as life itself."

The canyons are places for people of independence, from Indian hunters and farmers, to ranchers like Joe Biddlecome and Pearl Baker, to backpackers and wilderness zealots like writer Edward Abbey. These people hold in common more than they know. Like the environmentalists, those "dudes from Boston," Pearl Baker is saddened by the drowning of Glen Canyon: "I cried my eyes out over Lake Powell. I lived at Hite. So much has been lost that can never be regained. Never."

The trouble is this: at the same time that we set aside national parks and wilderness areas, we are developing this region economically. The canyons and mesas endure a never-ending series of threats to their integrity, some successful and some turned back—for a time. They have been used or they are proposed for use as sites for dams, open-pit coal mines, oil fields, power plants, uranium mines, and nuclear waste dumps. Roads and powerlines crisscross the Colorado Plateau in ever-denser networks. Somewhere between the distant poles of opinion held by those who hope to save as much open land as possible and those who will use it to turn a quick profit there must lie a balance, a reasonable compromise.

Clifford Duncan speaks of the Ute way:

Land is like a shrine. If you change it, you are competing with the Creator of the world. The Indian way is to follow but don't get ahead. So no one has the right to move rivers. No one has a right to make dams.

The Hill Creek extension of the reservation, south along the east bank of the Green River—it's our wilderness area. A lot of our tribal members use it for hunting. When I go out there, it's a remaking of me again. Because that's where I came from. If you leave a little spot for me somewhere that's never been bothered, that would be all we need. It's almost like rechargeable batteries — I get recharged.

Somehow I have to keep myself in a straight line. I need that. Indian people need that.

Hail pommels the rocky promontory of Dead Horse Point State Park on the northeast border of Canyonlands National Park. This spit of land overlooking the Colorado River two thousand feet below was used by cowboys as a natural corral for wild mustangs.

Along with whatever else may be needed from the canyons, all people need that.

FROM THE ZENITH

As John Wesley Powell and his men floated between Cataract and Glen canyons on the Colorado River in 1869, the last unnamed mountain range in the United States appeared downcanyon. Fred Dellenbaugh described this view on the second Powell expedition in 1871:

We could see through to the end of the canyon. ...The world seemed suddenly to open out before us, and in the middle of it, clear and strong against a sky of azure, accented by the daylight moon, stood the Unknown Mountains ... weird and silent in their untrodden mystery.

Powell named these five isolated volcanic peaks the Henry Mountains. Other mountain archipelagoes dot the inner Canyon Country. Slickrock and sandhills roll for dozens of miles on level mesas and plateaus, and from this sere desert sea the mountains rise like islands. The La Sals, Abajos, Ute Mountain, the Carrizos, and Navajo Mountain all surround the Henrys in a great semicircle across the Four Corners.

These mountains and the highest of the plateaus stand at the zenith of Canyon Country. They are stanchions for the sky, rising as monumental guardians over the maze of rock that falls away from them. They become familiar and reassuring when spotted at a distance, and traveling across the Canyon Country one rarely passes beyond sight of them. They tether us to the earth and define the horizon. Indian people call the mountains sacred and bound their world with them.

The Henrys remain both the best and least known of these mountains. To most, they are unknown, but to geologists all over the world they are a "classic field area," the defining example of a category of mountains called laccoliths.

Beneath laccolithic mountains, molten rock rises toward the earth's surface but does not erupt or reach a vent. Rising in ponds below ground—laccolith means "rock pond"—the lava domes the rocks above, creating mountains. In the Henrys, the La Sals, and the Abajos, erosion has stripped away most of the sedimentary formations, exposing the central core of dark volcanic rock. The unmistakable blue dome of Navajo Mountain seems to be a laccolith still shielded by a bubble of sandstone.

W. H. Holmes, working with the Wheeler Survey in 1874 and 1875, first recognized the Henrys as laccoliths. But it was Powell's associate, Grove Karl Gilbert, who mapped them in detail and worked out their geology. More than sixty years later, Charles B. Hunt expanded on Gilbert's work using the techniques of a new generation of U.S. Geological Survey scientists. In 1936, when Hunt was working on the Henrys' two smallest peaks, known as the Little Rockies, his packer needed six days to take the horses back to the road head at Trachyte Ranch, maneuver a truck through the clay and sand to Green River for supplies, and return to camp. Charlie Hunt remembers those days:

In the 1930s the area still was frontier — a long distance from railroads, paved roads, telephones, stores, or medical services. This was not Marlboro country: it was Bull Durham country. The geological work had to be done by packtrain — about the last of the big packtrain surveys in the West, and the end of an era. We didn't have air photos; we didn't have topographic maps. We went into the Henry Mountains with a white sheet of paper. All I had was a copy of the 1875 map made by the Powell Survey and Gilbert's field notebooks. Following in his tracks, I learned by his doing, not from what he said. Gilbert is my greatest teacher.

In Canyon Country, volcanic rocks often mean high elevation. Mount Peale in the laccolithic La Sals reaches 12,721 feet, the highest point on the Colorado Plateau. Erosion-resistant basalt caps the High Plateaus in western Utah, many of which stand 11,000 feet high, their flat summits glaciated during the Pleistocene epoch, a few tens of thousands of years ago.

Over the last twenty million years, uplift and faulting has created a "grand staircase" of High Plateaus, a series of cliffs made from rock formations younger at each step toward the top. At the high rims of these planed-off mountains, in the soft Wasatch Formation, the slow but persistent efforts of snow, rain, wind, and gravity have sculpted magnificent amphitheaters, as at Bryce Canyon and Cedar Breaks.

The Paiute Indians once lived here, wintering low with the rabbits, moving up with the deer in spring, "like white men do today with their livestock," says Southern Paiute elder Clifford Jake. The Paiute were masters at harvesting the land. Their traditional diet reads like a regional checklist of plants and animals: mesquite beans, yucca fruits, sego lily roots, cholla cactus blossoms, prickly pears, roasted agave hearts, Indian ricegrass seeds, piñon nuts, pine sap, acorns, serviceberries, juniper berries, quail, grasshoppers, ants, pronghorn, chipmunks, lizards, porcupines.

The Colorado Plateau begins at the western foot of the High Plateaus, at St. George, Cedar City, and Richfield, Utah. Move eastward and you go cross-grain against the faultlines, climbing up and over the great Hurricane Cliffs and the White Cliffs of Zion to the Pink Cliffs of Bryce. You intersect the Virgin and Sevier river valleys, green with fields and village oases.

At the eastern edges of the High Plateaus on the rim of the Aquarius, along the Boulder Mountain Road above Capitol Reef, you look out over slickrock — a desert of stone, red and golden and desert-varnished. From the Paunsaugunt Plateau, you see Bryce Canyon, the jewel at the zenith of Canyon Country.

In winter, snow mantles the rim of the Paunsaugunt. Below, the world drops away to the russet and orange and creamy-pink spires of Bryce Canyon and the dazzle of melting snow. At night, snowdrifts sparkle like fine crystal, competing in brilliance with the clarity of the moonstruck air and the stars themselves.

The Paiute say that Coyote found the Legend People misbehaving in this place and turned them into rocks, creating *Unka-timpe-wa-wince-pock-ich*, "Red rocks standing like men in a bowl-shaped canyon." More recent residents named the place for Mormon pioneer Ebenezer Bryce.

The Pollock family of Tropic helped Ebenezer, a consumptive, run his cattle. They fenced Bryce's cattle below Sunset Point and always claimed Bryce was too pious a man to have uttered the famous quip attributed to him about his namesake canyon: "It's a hell of a place to lose a cow."

The current scion of the Pollocks is Herman, who believes in the divine ordination of national parks in southern Utah:

These national parks have a divine purpose. They are not here by chance; they were foreordained. They were found by my own people, by the Latter-day Saints who came to Utah to find Zion. And they have brought the world to rub shoulders with the peculiar people who came here and found them. They are fulfilling a destiny — to remove the animosity of the world coming here to see these splendors.

Herm Pollock remembers riding up into Bryce to Sunset Point in 1913 on his father's livestock trail. He can still hear his father whistling happily across the range in 1928, bringing the news, "We've got a national park." He guided Dr. Herbert Gregory when he came to map geology at Bryce Canyon; he sang cowboy songs at Ruby's Inn in 1938. Today, Herm still sings his songs and tells his stories to summer tourists at the Inn, nearly fifty years after he started and some years after retiring from a long career working in Canyon Country national parks.

Pollock argues unequivocally that the Canyon Country scenery all was created by a three-hour earthquake, a "colossal cataclysm," in 34 A.D. Although geologists might disagree with Pollock about some of these landscapes, they do agree about others. The Canyon Country has seen some cataclysms.

Volcanic activity has poured molten rock over the rim of the Grand Canyon near Toroweap Point, covered the tops of the High Plateaus with lava flows, and left "necks" standing where the outer cones of volcanoes have worn away. Although a volcano eroded to its central throat becomes a smaller mountain, it remains a mountain: Agatha in Monument Valley rises more than a thousand feet; mighty Shiprock in northwestern New Mexico — the Navajo's "Rock with Wings" — rises still higher, to 7,178 feet.

The Colorado Plateau averages five thousand feet above sea level, and a woodland of piñon pine and juniper, affectionately known as "p-j," covers its intermediate-elevation mesas. In winter, snow dusts the woodland and leaves a tiny pillow of icy fluff on each juniper berry. Summers are hot and difficult; only gnats break the silence of air heavy with heat. San Juan County, Utah, with record temperatures ranging from minus 29 degrees to 115 degrees Fahrenheit, is typical.

The mountain lion — or cougar or puma (the cat is known by forty common names) — roams throughout the Canyon Country but is rarely seen. Shy and primarily nocturnal, the cougar feeds on deer, foxes, rabbits, mice, and occasionally livestock.

26

Requiring about twelve inches of annual precipitation, the woodland marks the baseline for mapping Canyon Country plant communities. Below lies drier country: desert grasslands and shrublands, where a single clump of wildflowers becomes a major find—a garden in itself. These arid places may catch only five inches of moisture yearly, but they do not cover enough continuous land to qualify as an official North American desert. The primary definition of Canyon Country remains geological.

Above the short forest of piñon and juniper, authentic mountain trees take over. First comes ponderosa, the fragrant orange-barked, long-needled pine of the Grand Canyon's rims and lower mountain slopes everywhere in the Southwest. Abert's squirrels live here. Their chatter guarantees identification of the pine. On the Kaibab Plateau, the squirrels have been isolated long enough to develop a unique race with white tails and black bellies.

Still higher, Douglas fir, spruce, aspen, and subalpine fir cloak mountains and plateaus between eighty-five hundred and twelve thousand feet. The tops of the High Plateaus, in particular, nourish lovely stands of aspen and lush wildflower meadows, easily reached at Cedar Breaks. These subalpine forests are the wettest places in Canyon Country. Much of their annual forty inches of moisture comes as snow, and the growing season may barely exceed ten weeks in late summer.

Bristlecone pines mark the treeline, though the gnarled Rocky Mountain species hugging the rims above Cedar Breaks does not live as long as the five-thousand-year-old Great Basin bristlecones farther west. Finally, above twelve thousand feet, come fragments of Rocky Mountain alpine tundra found in Canyon Country only on the La Sals and the highest of the High Plateaus, Mounts Delano and Belknap on the Tushar Plateau.

Below these tiny patches of alpine tundra, forests mantle the zenith. Within these forests grow sacred medicines used by the Indian peoples. "These herbs are gifts from the Holy People, to restore life," says Steve Darden of the Navajo tradition. "In our medicine bundles we have earth, plants, and tobacco from each of our four sacred mountains."

Each mountain rising from the vast level surface of the Colorado Plateau focuses attention. We may understand much of their biology and geology, but in their height, grace, and power, these are still unknown mountains.

As Steve Darden says:

The Holy People live in the mountains. There's life there. There's beauty. There's spirit. And if you've ever seen clouds there you see that mountain like a hand grasping those clouds, a handshake between Mother Earth and Father Sky. There's life up there. That's why it's sacred.

One hundred and eighty million years ago, great sweeps of sand like those at Coral Pink Sand Dunes State Reserve, southeast of Zion National Park, covered much of the Southwest. Gradually, the sediment solidifying above the dunes compressed them into massive sandstone formations.

FROM THE NADIR

Voices from throughout the Canyon Country come together deep in the Grand Canyon of the Colorado River. Except for the Virgin River, which joins the Colorado below the Canyon, and the Sevier, which flows into the Great Basin, every arroyo, stream, and river on the Colorado Plateau leads into the nadir, into what naturalist John Burroughs called "the divine abyss."

In 1869, John Wesley Powell was looking for blank places on maps where he could make a name for himself. He found them along the Colorado. Powell started his river exploits in Wyoming, on the Green, and explored Dinosaur, Canyonlands, and Glen Canyon. But these were preliminaries. John Wesley Powell is forever linked to the Grand Canyon.

Powell had formidable energy and restlessness; they carried him into trouble, but they carried him through trouble, too. His intelligence equalled his physical energy. Our image of Powell comes from formal portraits taken in his maturity; when he led his men through the canyons he was just thirty-five years old.

Powell lost his right arm in the Battle of Shiloh, but his tenacity carried him through another two years of Civil War battles. He was known as "the Major" ever after. When he started hauling his geology students from Illinois State Normal University to the West for field trips in 1867, he was advancing his own informal scientific training as much as theirs. Summer wanderings by students still could pass muster as real explorations, and to Powell's delight "firsts" filled their trips.

Two years later, in 1869, he made his first passage through the canyons of the Colorado, again with a company of untrained men, and became the first to document the innermost canyon world. Trappers, prospectors, and military expeditions had seen parts of this world before him, but Powell connected the river to the rest of mapped reality.

On the seventieth day out from Green River, Wyoming, he and his men camped at the confluence of the Colorado and San Juan rivers. The calm water and sandstone cathedrals of Glen Canyon soothed them after their harrowing days in Lodore, Desolation, and Cataract canyons, and Powell wrote:

...past these towering monuments, past these mounded billows of orange sandstone, past these oak-set glens, past these fern-decked alcoves, past these mural caves, we glide hour after hour, stopping now and then, as our attention is arrested by some new wonder....

They needed the rest. Another month remained of their voyage, and after just four days more in Glen Canyon, they reached the mouth of the Paria and saw below them the river cutting into the limestone that "bodes toil and danger." They entered Marble Gorge, and the Grand Canyon swallowed them, spitting them out 279 river miles later, minus three men. These three left the expedition in despair over unrelenting rapids and dwindling rations, only to be killed by Paiutes who believed them to be as potentially troublesome as the prospectors who had recently murdered a Hualapai woman across the river.

Powell and his men ran the river twice, returning in 1871 and going as far as Kanab Creek, halfway through Grand Canyon. Powell's journal still makes powerful reading, even when his exaggerated style gets in the way of his facts. But no matter the quibbles; Powell's men were trailblazers. Not for many years would Colorado river-runners learn enough to avoid the unnerving rides, the toilsome lining and portaging, and the spills that ruined food and equipment.

John Wesley Powell turned his curiosity and intensity loose in Canyon Country for a few years, spun out a series of bold geologic ideas, and then moved on to Washington, D.C., where he helped establish the United States Geological Survey. He left behind a group of remarkable associates who filled out his ideas. They went to work in the churning wake of the Major and solidified his legacy.

One of them, Clarence Dutton, published his masterwork, *Tertiary History of the Grand Canyon District*, in 1882, barely ten years after Powell's river expeditions. Dutton made the Grand Canyon his own. He called it: "The sublimest thing on earth. It is so … by virtue of the whole—its *ensemble*."

Both in his science and his prose, Dutton succeeded as well as anyone in understanding this complex landscape. He warned others who would try to fathom the Grand Canyon:

> A perpetual glamour envelops the landscape. Things are not what they seem, and the perceptions cannot tell us what they are. … As the mind strives to realize [the Canyon's] proportions, its spirit is broken and its imagination is completely crushed.

Some people dared to pass Dutton's threshold of understanding and made the Grand Canyon the focus of their lives. Others tried to live there as they would anywhere—but the Canyon always fooled them, casting what Dutton called its "spell of enchantment," leaving behind a "troubled sense of immensity."

The immensity always is there. It is a presence, an abstract concept elsewhere that here you can see. Some never cease to find it "troubling." For others, there is something companionable about such vastness.

Adventurers have been drawn to the Colorado River in Grand Canyon for more than a century since Powell. In 1890, Robert Brewster Stanton surveyed a water-level railroad line, which was never built. Ellsworth and Emery Kolb made motion pictures of their 1911 trip and showed these movies at their little studio perched on the South Rim for the next sixty years. In 1937, Buzz Holmstrom became the first person to run the Canyon solo and he tried hard to hold true to its lesson of humility:

> I have already had my reward, in the doing of the things, the stars, cliffs and canyons, the roar of the rapids, the moon, the uncertainty and worry, the relief …

Nowhere is the contrast between the Colorado and the arid canyon walls it carves through more vivid than in Grand Canyon. A river trip overwhelms you with the difference between wet and dry. And nowhere does the scale of the river and the canyons come as clear as it does when you "swim" a small rapid, bobbing through the waves to get the feel of your life vest in case your raft flips in Horn Creek or Sockdolager Rapids and you *have* to swim. Surrounded by the cold water of the river, you feel small and fragile, but joyfully alive.

Along the river, side canyons lead up to hidden paradises: alcoves with still pools and exotic touches of fern and monkeyflower. At Havasu Creek, the water itself seems extravagant, its milky blue-green (colored by travertine) tumbling down past the home of the Havasupai Indians, over cascades and waterfalls, through tangles of wild grape, to mingle with the Colorado—a barbaric stream by comparison.

In 1948, fewer than one hundred people had run the Colorado River through the Grand Canyon. By 1954, the total had reached two hundred. But in the 1950s and 1960s, commercial river-running companies flourished. In 1972, more than sixteen thousand people ran the river in one year and it became clear the Colorado had to be managed. Or rather, the *people* had to be managed; the river already was, for the headgates closed at Glen Canyon Dam in 1963, transforming the river world of Grand Canyon all the way to Lake Mead.

In the 1930s, Glen Canyon was the centerpiece of a mammoth proposed park. Escalante National Park, named after the Spanish Franciscan who traversed the Canyon Country in 1776, would have preserved seven thousand square miles of southeastern Utah. During hearings on the proposal, Charlie Hunt testified before Congress as a geologic expert; few other scientists knew the canyons away from the river. He spoke enthusiastically about the park but felt Congress was a little uneasy, even in those days, about its size: "It was too big a piece of country to take out completely from use." Toward the end of the 1930s, other matters took precedence in Washington, D.C., and Escalante National Park died on the desk of the Secretary of the Interior.

Twenty years later, Congress legislated other uses for Glen Canyon. As a result, the Colorado River now disappears in Lake Powell, the reservoir backed up behind Glen Canyon Dam. One hundred and eighty miles downstream, the river reemerges below the dam, its volume controlled not by spring runoff from the Rocky Mountains but by computers programmed to serve power needs in distant cities.

The reservoir filled in 1980. Today the release of water into the Grand Canyon fluctuates drastically between 3,000 and 30,000 cubic feet per second (cfs), although in 1983 Mother Nature took over from the computers and heavy runoff forced emergency releases of 100,000 cfs. That year, young river-runners had an awesome taste of the old Colorado—"Big Red."

The triumph of the Colorado River and its many tributaries is the Grand Canyon, the most complex and intricate system of canyons, gorges, and ravines in the world. This spectacular network extends from Lees Ferry, at the head of Marble Gorge, near the northern border of Arizona, to the Grand Wash Cliffs near the Nevada line, a distance of 279 miles.

Steven Carothers, a research biologist for Grand Canyon National Park, has been studying Grand Canyon ecology since the first National Park Service research river trip in 1968. He now works in the canyon surveying fish populations by electrofishing at night, when the fish cannot see his boat approaching. Carothers has run every stretch of the river but Lava Falls and Crystal Rapid in the dark: "At night the whole river becomes the same unknown Powell must have felt. But we just catch glimpses of that uncertainty and fear, because we always know when a rapid will be over. Powell didn't have that luxury."

Today water releases must be balanced to maintain enough flow for river-running, for power generation, for delivery of irrigation and drinking water to the lower Colorado River Basin, for threatened native fish and birds like humpback chub and Bell's vireo, for a trophy trout fishery, for preserving the river's sediment load and camping beaches—and for a hundred other resource needs we can define and a thousand we cannot.

Steve Carothers says:

> Our task is to guess right, to project and to predict, based on what we can see now. It's real dangerous because we don't have the whole story yet; we need another fifty years.

The management Carothers talks about involves hundreds of miles of river—180 miles of Lake Powell, 240 miles of the free-flowing Colorado above Lake Mead in Grand Canyon, and, downstream, a series of reservoirs all the way to the sea. Few people can think in such terms. Even fewer can comprehend the time scale of the Grand Canyon.

The Grand Canyon confounds comprehension. A little more than a century after Powell and Dutton studied it, we still cannot say exactly how old it is or how it formed. The river has flowed in Marble Gorge for thirty million years, according to the evidence in the rocks. But after the Colorado meets the Little Colorado River, it inexplicably turns west and cuts more than six thousand feet deep through the Kaibab Plateau, slicing its way through to some of the most ancient rock exposed on the continent: 1.7-billion-year-old Vishnu Schist, rock that makes the "old" canyon above seem downright youthful.

Geologists also know that the river could not have flowed through the Grand Wash Cliffs where it leaves the western end of Grand Canyon until about six million years ago. The rocks say that conclusively. So not until then could the Colorado River achieve its present course in Grand Canyon. The Gulf of California did not exist until four or five million years ago, so drainage beyond the Colorado Plateau remains completely mysterious.

We do not yet have a widely-accepted story that ties these facts up in a neat package, and this seems appropriate. The Grand Canyon will never be a neat package.

In the Paria Primitive Area near Kanab, Utah, the yellow blossoms of Mormon tea brighten a desert landscape. Before its use as a beverage by early Mormons, various southwest Indian tribes employed the plant for medicinal purposes.

The Hopis understand this. Hopi artist Michael Kabotie says: "The Grand Canyon is symbolic of the womb just like the kiva is a symbol for the womb. And when you die, you go back through the Grand Canyon to the underworld." The Hopis believe their ancestors entered this world through the Grand Canyon. Today's Hopi people still make pilgrimages to the sipapu, the sacred spring in the Grand Canyon where this entrance took place. For the Hopi, life has both its beginning and its end in the Grand Canyon.

Steve Carothers talks about his feelings for the Canyon:

> Every year now for as long as I can remember, we have run the river in December. That's my favorite time. Nobody else is there. It's incredibly peaceful. And incredibly demanding—just to keep your hands warm. It takes that combination of extremes—the physical as well as the intellectual, the entire animal—to put all of the pieces together. Everything gets whole. I can't find that world without boundaries anywhere but Grand Canyon.

THE SEVENTH DIRECTION

Somewhere within these six directions lies the center, the heart of Canyon Country.

Edward Abbey mused about this heart of the canyonlands in his book, *Beyond the Wall:*

> There was a time when, in my search for essences, I concluded that the canyonland country has no heart. I was wrong. The canyonlands did have a heart, a living heart, and that heart was Glen Canyon and the golden, flowing Colorado River.

Navajo people define the heart as the seventh direction. Anywhere in the Canyon Country, anywhere between their sacred mountains, can be the center. It is wherever we are, right now within the six directions: the point of balance. Steve Darden calls it "a feeling and a reassurance."

Navajos celebrate this balance every day in their prayers:

> With beauty before me, I walk
> With beauty behind me, I walk
> With beauty above me, I walk
> With beauty below me, I walk
>
> From the East beauty has been restored
> From the South beauty has been restored
> From the West beauty has been restored
> From the North beauty has been restored
> From the zenith in the sky beauty has been restored
> From the nadir of the earth beauty has been restored
> From all around me beauty has been restored.

From the six directions come beauty and harmony, what the Navajo call *hózhó*. Daily restored to us, *hózhó* is alive all around us in this place called Canyon Country.

ZION

■ *Above:* Spring rains and snowmelt fill potholes along the eastern border of Zion National Park. These natural reservoirs both sustain and create a myriad of life forms. ■ *Right:* Zion's Mount Isaac is the result of sand-laden winds that blew across the land over millions of years, depositing enormous dunes that gradually cemented into rock.

■ *Left:* A late March snowstorm dusts the Great White Throne, a prominent landmark in Zion National Park. In the High Plateaus above Zion, average precipitation is twenty-five inches per year. ■ *Above:* The West Temple contains seven of the eight sedimentary rock formations found in Zion, from the ancient Moenkopi Formation to the much younger Carmel. The limestones and sandstones of the Carmel Formation came from the long-vanished Sundance Sea.

■ *Above:* Zion's beloved Watchman, as seen from the park's western border town of Springdale, radiates an orange glow at sunset. ■ *Right:* Canyon maple leaves contrast vividly with a parched streambed. Buried underneath may be the eggs of tadpole shrimp, which are laid in water and must wait for water to hatch. The hardiest eggs can survive up to twenty-five years.

■ *Left:* The Virgin River Narrows, so named because canyon walls are little more than sixteen feet apart in sections of the upper gorge, drops thirteen miles, from the top of the Markagunt Plateau down into Zion Canyon. ■ *Above:* Some call the less-known Kolob region the "hidden showcase of Zion." ■ *Overleaf:* A winter scene in the heart of Zion Canyon evokes California's Yosemite Valley. Unlike Yosemite, which was carved by a glacier, Zion was cut primarily by the Virgin River.

In the higher elevations of Zion's Kolob region, in the north-west, stands of aspen border hillsides speckled with spruce and fir. Within the park's 147,000 acres lie four major plant zones, ranging from desert to forest. They extend from altitudes of less than four thousand to nearly nine thousand feet.

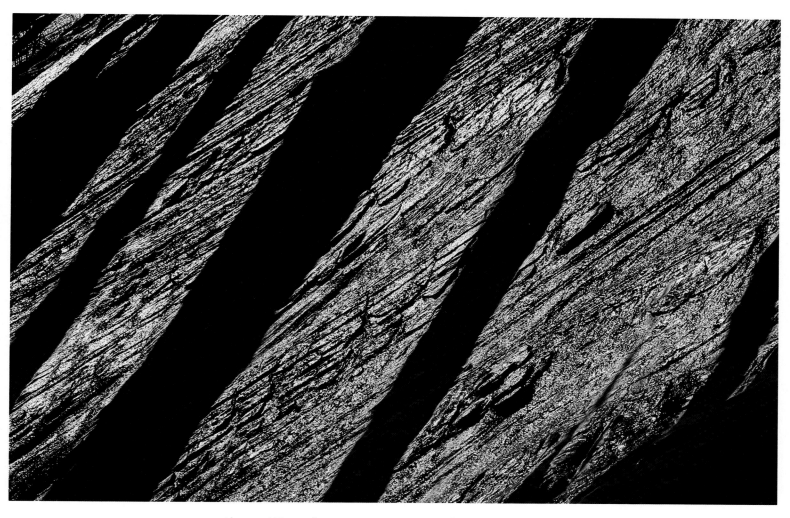

■ *Above:* Water from a spring rain rushes down a wall of porous, cross-bedded Navajo Sandstone on the trail to Angel's Landing. ■ *Overleaf:* Southeast of Zion National Park, Coral Pink Sand Dunes State Reserve recalls an era 180 million years ago when sand covered almost the entire Colorado Plateau, creating a desert vast enough to rival the Sahara.

■ *Above:* A moonrise over the Watchman in Zion National Park bespeaks a serenity common to the park today, but not always characteristic of the region. Great floods, droughts, windstorms, and violent upheavals have recurred periodically through the ages. ■ *Right:* A gambel oak leaf traces a path in the Coral Pink Sand Dunes State Reserve, where summer temperatures sometimes exceed 115 degrees Fahrenheit.

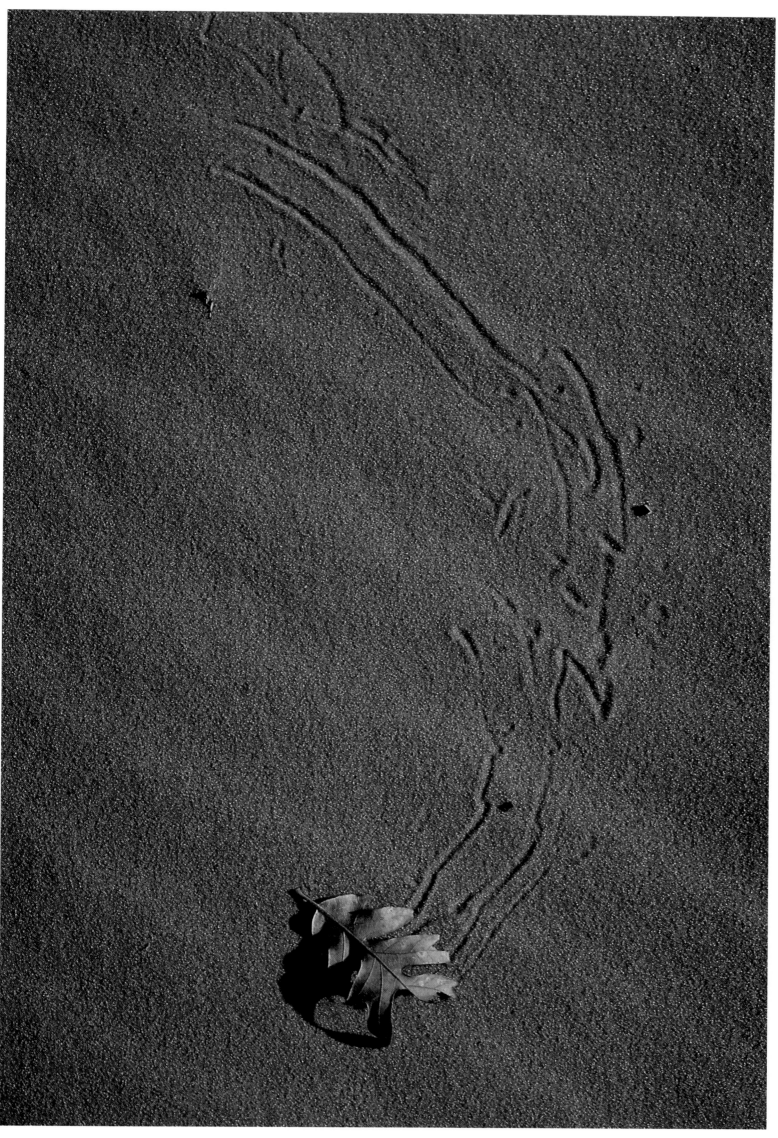

■ *Left:* The spirit of warmheartedness glows in the face of Lorena Roundy, known in the Zion area for her intricate netting work. ■ *Above:* Prime grazing land abuts Zion. From 1861 to 1909, Mormon settlers grazed cattle and sheep on the canyon floor, until President William Taft proclaimed Mukuntuweap, "straight canyon," a national monument. Ten years later in 1919, Mukuntuweap became Zion National Park.

BRYCE & CEDAR BREAKS

■ *Above:* Bryce Canyon National Park lies on the rim of the Paunsaugunt Plateau, one of the High Plateaus of Canyon Country. ■ *Right:* Nearby Cedar Breaks National Monument cuts back into the Markagunt Plateau, which lies two thousand feet above Bryce. These two plateaus, which range in elevation from nine thousand to over eleven thousand feet, contain rock formations less than seventy million years old. This is considered young in geologic time.

■ *Left:* Limestone and siltstone compose Bryce Canyon's walls and pinnacles. Part of the Wasatch Formation, these deposits were laid down in a sixty million-year-old lake that once covered the landscape. ■ *Above:* Water and ice sculpted many of Bryce's towering shapes and windowed cliffs.

■ *Above:* A lanky column holds center stage in the sparsely vegetated soil below Bryce's Sunset Point. ■ *Right:* Climbing the switchbacks that lead in and out of Bryce Canyon is arduous even by horseback. ■ *Overleaf:* The pinks, yellows, mauves, and umbers illuminating Bryce are derived chiefly from iron and manganese, which reflect the sun's shifting rays.

■ *Above:* On an early winter's day, the only sounds likely to emanate from Bryce Canyon are the sounds of erosion: the cracking of fissures or the falling of rocks from limestone walls.
■ *Right:* Hikers on Bryce's Navajo Trail must pass through the monstrous shadow of a gargoyle in stone. The Paiute who hunted in Bryce described the rock forms with a word meaning "red rocks standing like men in a bowl-shaped canyon."

■ *Left:* Throughout Bryce Canyon, hard beds of sandstone and cemented gravel provide protective caps for the softer and more easily eroded limestone beneath. Eventually, the limestone dissolves and the walls and towers collapse. ■ *Above:* Wrangler Tom Richards, who has lived near Bryce all his life, guides horses and visitors in and out of the canyon.

■ *Above:* Everything from canned tuna to T-squares and .22s is sold at the dry-goods store in Escalante, Utah, northeast of Bryce. ■ *Right:* A tombstone in Grafton, to the south, recalls the area's pioneer days. It was in 1866 that Mormons in pursuit of a band of marauding Indians first came upon the Pink Cliffs of Bryce Canyon. Named for one of its early homesteaders, Ebenezer Bryce, a Mormon convert from Scotland, the canyon became a national park in 1928.

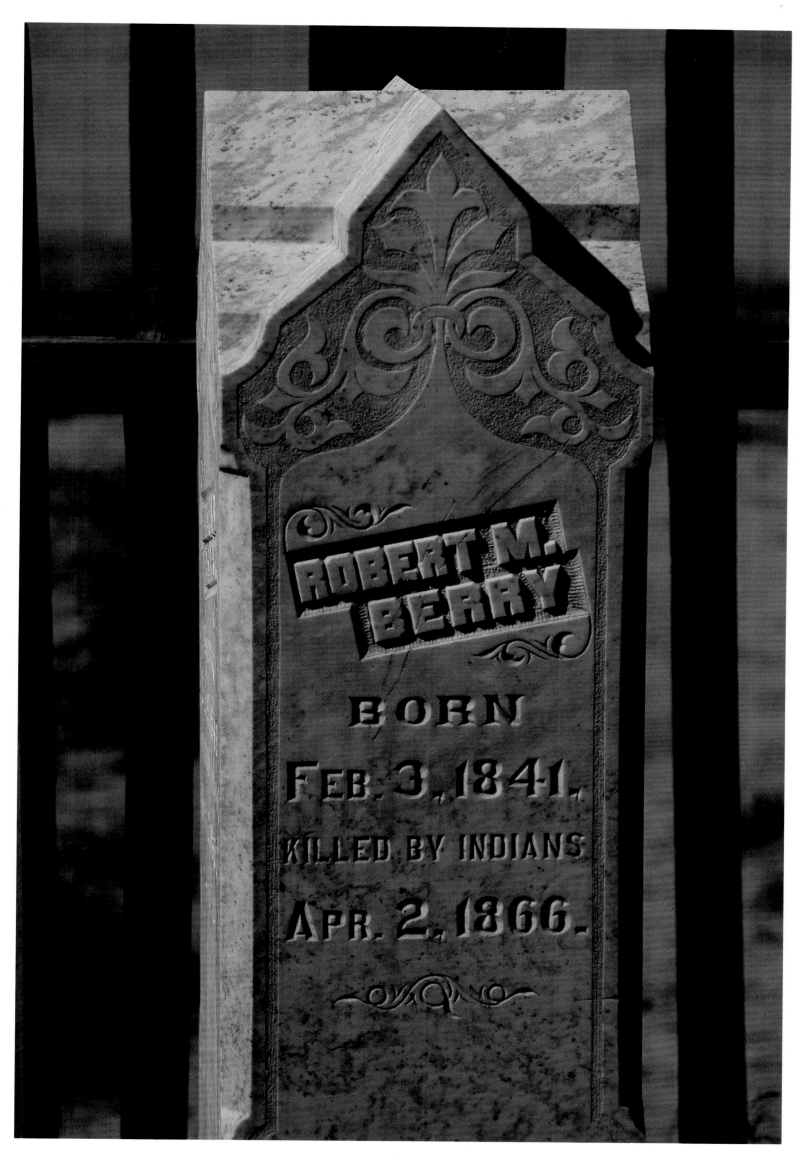

CAPITOL REEF

■ *Left:* Quaking aspen—the most widely distributed tree in North America—dominates the hillsides along the Boulder Mountain Road leading from Escalante to Capitol Reef National Park. ■ *Above:* Navajo Dome, in the north-central section of Capitol Reef National Park, brings to mind a similar dome-shaped structure in Washington, D.C. Such domes gave the park the word Capitol in its name.

■ *Above:* Orchards at Capitol Reef National Park dazzle autumn visitors. ■ *Right:* Long before the Mormons planted the area with fruit trees, the Fremont Indians were drawn to this fertile Fremont River watershed. ■ *Overleaf:* Capitol Reef includes a remarkable hundred-mile-long geologic phenomenon known as the Waterpocket Fold. The steeply tilted rocks of the fold are long, narrow, eroded "reefs," part of which forms a single, steep, S-shaped curve.

■ *Left:* The eastern backdrop for the Waterpocket Fold, the Henry Mountains were the last range in the lower forty-eight states to be mapped. ■ *Above:* The mule deer, named for its large ears, feeds on acorns, berries, cactus fruits, and grasses. ■ *Overleaf:* An aerial view of the badlands east of Capitol Reef shows the mazelike drainage patterns in Mancos Shale.

■ *Above:* On the Fremont River Highway east of Capitol Reef, sunset silhouettes a tumulus of Mancos Shale against a wall of titian orange. ■ *Right:* The unpaved Burr Trail, the only road across the southern Waterpocket Fold, winds down precipitously from the fold's crest. ■ *Overleaf:* A magnificent sandstone escarpment towers above what was originally the Mormon town of Fruita and its lush orchards, and is now Capitol Reef National Park's main campground.

■ *Left:* The sinuous, monoclinal Waterpocket Fold is the result of horizontal layers of sedimentary rock tilting and then buckling during the long, slow uplift of the Colorado Plateau some sixty million years ago. ■ *Above:* Vegetation is scarce on the dry slopes of the fold. Piñon pine and Utah juniper grow in the fissures of the sandstone walls.

■ *Above:* A Great Basin rattlesnake is reflected in a water-pocket. Like other snakes, rattlers cannot tolerate extreme temperatures. In summer, they become nocturnal, avoiding the heat of the day in protected shelters. In winter, they hibernate in rock slides or crevices. ■ *Right:* A colorful tapestry of maple leaves serves as a graceful reminder of the changing seasons.

ARCHES

■ *Left:* Landscape Arch in Arches National Park was once a solid wall of sandstone called a fin. When erosion wears away at a recess in a fin, a hole appears and gradually enlarges.
■ *Above:* Like huge dinosaur bones, fins sprawl across the park's northern section, which is known as Devil's Garden.
■ *Overleaf:* The park's prized Delicate Arch is aptly named. In the life cycle of an arch, Delicate is old and will one day topple.

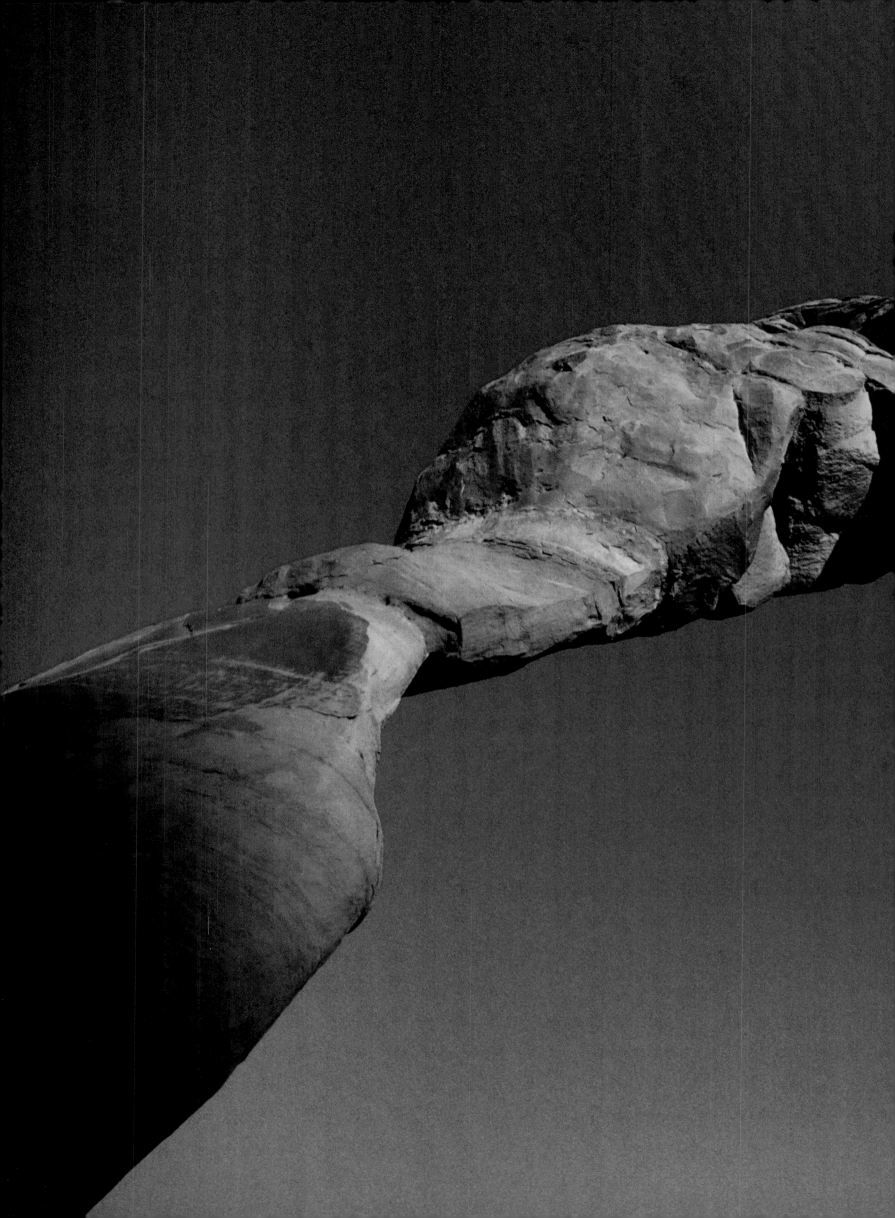

Landscape Arch, one of the longest natural spans in the world, measures 291 feet — nearly the length of a football field. It stands 106 feet tall, but is only 11 feet wide at its narrowest point and 6 feet thick at its thinnest. A journalist gave the arch its name because it so elegantly frames the landscape.

■ *Above:* Skyline Arch near Devil's Garden Campground more than doubled in size in 1940, when a great block of sandstone fell out of its opening. Before that, it was called "Arch-in-the-Making." ■ *Overleaf:* Dawn irradiates Delicate Arch, a model of sheer grace and power, beauty and endurance. The symbol of Arches National Park, it stands forty-five feet tall.

A snowstorm over Broken Arch (a misnomer — the rock is cracked but not severed) highlights the desert varnish that coats the arch like frosting. Ranging in color from dark red to black, desert varnish derives from manganese and iron oxides. These minerals require sufficient precipitation and high evaporation rates to develop into the thick, glossy patina.

In the southern Courthouse Towers section of Arches National Park stands the Tower of Babel, a stark monument to the ravages of erosion. When Courthouse Wash and its tributaries flood, they isolate huge rock masses, which weather away into slender monoliths much like those in Monument Valley.

■ *Above:* The major sandstone formation that characterizes the walls and fins of Arches is called Entrada and dates from the Jurassic Period 150 million years ago. ■ *Right:* Balanced Rock is actually a mammoth hoodoo — a great pillar of horizontal layers of rock that erode at different rates. The massive boulder of hard Entrada slickrock which gives Balanced Rock its name weighs almost four thousand tons.

■ *Left:* Ensconced in Double-O Arch, hikers relax at twilight.
No records list the first white explorers, but rock art indicates
that Arches was an ancient hunting ground for both the Anasazi
and Fremont Indians. ■ *Above:* The moon rising over Delicate
Arch seems to hold the magic power of an amulet.

■ *Above:* A proud martyr to the elements, Delicate Arch straddles a basin of smooth Entrada Sandstone. Rain, snow, wind, changing temperatures, and gravity constantly wear away its stately structure. ■ *Right:* Devil's claw or fishhook cactus is named for its central spines, which are hooked at the tips. The shorter radial spines are straight and needle-sharp.

DINOSAUR

■ *Left:* Following a late spring hailstorm, a rainbow appears over Split Mountain in Dinosaur National Monument, located in northeast Utah and northwest Colorado. ■ *Above:* A main attraction at Dinosaur is the quarry-museum, where paleontologists, working since 1909, have uncovered a remarkable collection of mineralized dinosaur bones, including this skull of a *Camarasaurus.* ■ *Overleaf:* Split Mountain rises like a great white god over a field of grazing cattle.

The rocky knolls around Dinosaur National Monument attest to
a time when the Rocky Mountains began to rise. This area went
along for the ride. The mountain-building squeezed the rock
layers from the sides, warping and tilting them.

■ *Above:* Storm clouds whirl across the sky above Split Mountain Campground, twenty miles east of Vernal, Utah.
■ *Overleaf:* Snow-covered mountains rise from the Yampa Bench in the heart of Dinosaur National Monument. Some rocks in this region contain fossils of sea creatures that are two or three times the age of dinosaur fossils.

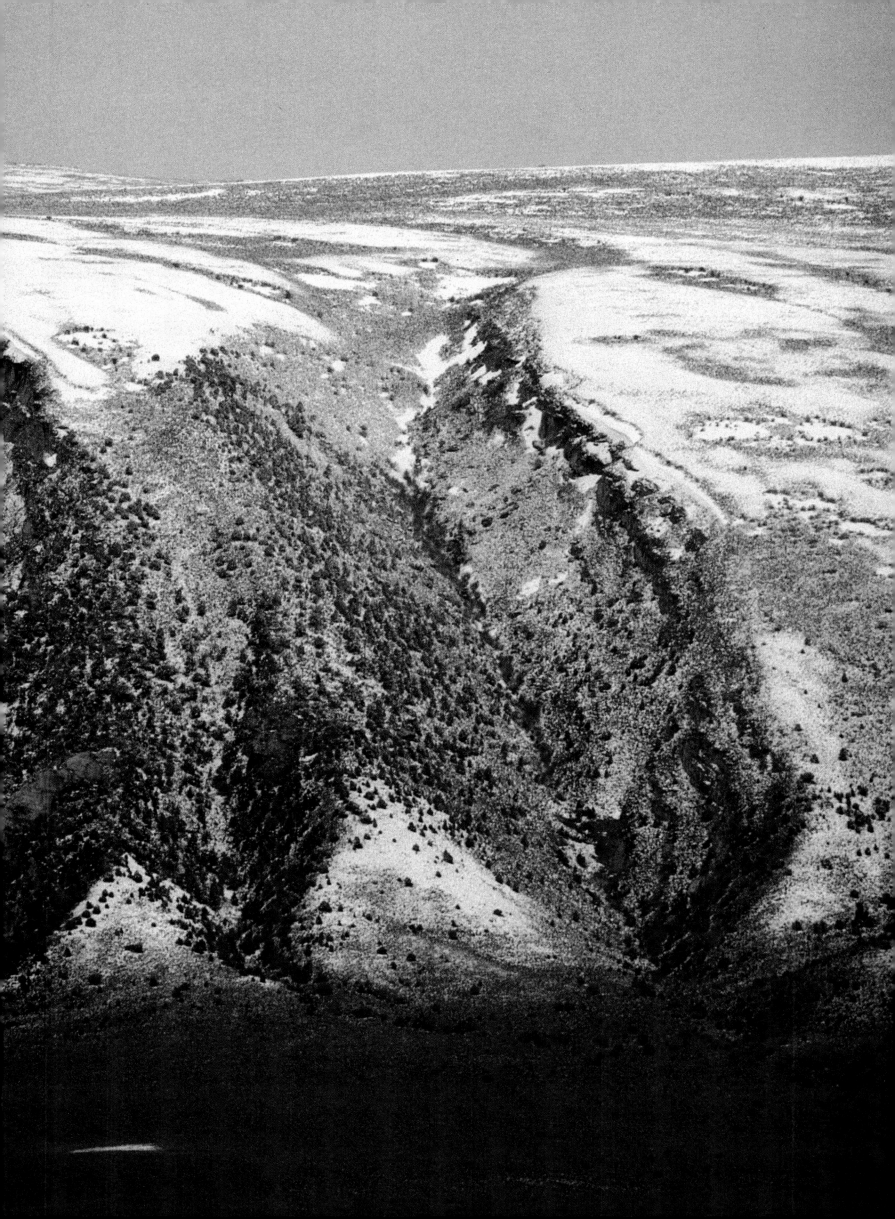

CANYONS OF COLORADO

■ *Above:* Along the Ute Trail in Colorado National Monument grow thickets of tamarisk and sagebrush. ■ *Right:* The lofty rock formations in Colorado National Monument are products of the Mesozoic Era—the age of dinosaurs—230 to 65 million years ago. In the center of Monument Canyon stands Independence Monument, 530 feet of Wingate Sandstone capped by a layer of denser, erosion-resistant Kayenta. The Book Cliffs in the far distance span the 150 miles between the towns of Grand Junction, Colorado, and Price, Utah.

■ *Left:* Splotches of lichen color the rocks at Black Canyon of the Gunnison National Monument in western Colorado. The Monument lies on the easternmost edge of the Colorado Plateau. ■ *Above:* The Gunnison River, a tributary of the Colorado, cuts a deep course through ancient Precambrian rock, whose dark and shadowy hue gives Black Canyon its name. Stripes on the canyon walls are the result of molten material forced into the cracks and joints of the base rock.

■ *Above:* Twice a year, cattle are herded to summer or winter range in the high plateaus and canyon valleys of the Colorado Plateau. ■ *Right:* A Mormon farmer and his wife pose with photographs of their family. The arid climate of the Colorado Plateau made farming a formidable and risky occupation even when the prehistoric Anasazi Indians lived here.

CANYONLANDS

■ *Left:* Dead Horse Point State Park overlooks the northeast section of Canyonlands National Park. With 337,570 acres of some of the wildest and most primitive country in the United States, Canyonlands enfolds the confluence of the Green and Colorado rivers deep within its maze of canyons. ■ *Above:* Along the slot section of the park's Joint Trail, colossal rocks overpower human forms. Slots occur at joints where water has sliced through fine-grained sandstone.

■ *Above:* An island butte rises out of a bedrock mesa north of Canyonlands National Park. ■ *Right:* Dawn illuminates Angel Arch, one of the park's most visited backcountry landmarks. The shadowed hoodoo in the foreground is called Molar Rock. ■ *Overleaf:* Dead Horse Point lies above a Colorado River gooseneck. The meandering pattern harks back to a time when the river flowed on a relatively flat plain, before the Colorado Plateau was uplifted and the river became entrenched.

■ *Above:* The same conditions which created the landscape at Arches—salt forcing its way up against overlying layers of rock and subsequent erosion—were at work in The Needles district of Canyonlands. ■ *Right:* A tempestuous sky reels above The Needles, on the east bank of rugged Cataract Canyon. ■ *Overleaf:* From atop the Abajo Mountains, southeast of Canyonlands National Park, one can look north to the La Sals, the highest peaks on the Colorado Plateau.

ANASAZI

■ *Left:* Prehistoric inhabitants of the Canyon Country, the Anasazi Indians left behind many remnants of their highly sophisticated culture. Built in the 1200s, Cliff Palace in Mesa Verde National Park in southwest Colorado is one of their most famous architectural achievements. ■ *Above:* An ancient volcanic plug known as Shiprock is a landmark of the Four Corners region, where most Anasazi ruins are concentrated.

A great kiva—an Anasazi social or religious center—lies at the heart of Pueblo Bonito in Chaco Canyon National Monument in northwest New Mexico. One of the largest prehistoric buildings in the Southwest, Pueblo Bonito rose to five stories and contained eight hundred rooms.

Contemporaries and often neighbors of the Anasazi, the Fremont Indians built few masonry pueblos—nothing as grand or sophisticated as the Anasazi dwellings. They did leave behind an impressive legacy of rock art, like this petroglyph of a bighorn sheep etched into a cliff wall.

■ *Above:* Anasazi people lived in Mummy Cave in Arizona's Canyon de Chelly National Monument from roughly 100 A.D. until they abandoned the canyon in the 1300s. ■ *Right:* Ruins such as these at Betatakin in Navajo National Monument help tell the Anasazi story. Archeologists believe the people living here migrated south to the Hopi mesas, while other Anasazi moved southeast toward the Rio Grande.

MONUMENT VALLEY

■ *Left:* A Navajo woman performs the final step in the long process of raising sheep and shearing, spinning, dyeing, and weaving wool. The Navajo, who call themselves *Diné,* The People, are descendants of nomadic Apacheans who migrated to the Canyon Country sometime after the Anasazi had abandoned it. ■ *Above:* The familiar East and West Mittens stand at the entranceway to Monument Valley Tribal Park, part of the sixteen million-acre Navajo Reservation, which is located in Utah, Arizona, and New Mexico.

■ *Above:* A hot-air balloon glides serenely along a sheer cliff wall in Monument Valley. The valley's prominent rock forms have attracted film and television producers since John Ford's 1938 movie, *Stagecoach.* ■ *Right:* A single star glows in the early morning twilight above Big Chief monument. ■ *Overleaf:* The desert landscape surrounding the red-rock monoliths of Monument Valley testifies to the age-old processes which turn sand into rock and back again into sand.

■ *Left:* Monument Valley's sandstone spires and towers are sometimes stately, sometimes amusing. The Totem Pole stands halfway along a seventeen-mile-long drive through the Tribal Park. ■ *Above:* This rocky triumvirate is known as the Three Sisters. ■ *Overleaf:* Sheep grazing near Artist's Point seem to cast their reflections in a fleecy sky. The Navajo took up sheep-raising after the Spanish introduced the animals in the 1500s.

Northwest of Monument Valley, the goosenecks of the San Juan River present classic examples of entrenched meanders. The silt-laden San Juan carved this thousand-foot-deep, winding chasm from the Hermosa and Cutler groups.

■ *Above:* The sandstone rock sculptures of Monument Valley are part of the Cutler Group, laid down roughly 260 million years ago. Today they go by such fanciful titles as "Stagecoach," "Bear and Rabbit," and "Castle Rock." Organ Rock Shale forms the pedestals of these sculptured monoliths.
■ *Overleaf:* Intermittent streams sculpt labyrinthine passageways in the sandstones of the Canyon Country.

GLEN CANYON

■ *Above:* The royal blue waters of Lake Powell, part of Glen Canyon National Recreation Area, spring from the combined forces of nature and technology. This 186-mile stretch of the Colorado River was turned into a huge reservoir with the completion of the Glen Canyon Dam in 1963. ■ *Right:* Here at historic Hole-in-the-Rock, Mormon pioneers struggled to cut a road through the steep rock walls of Glen Canyon, so they could ferry their wagons across the Colorado.

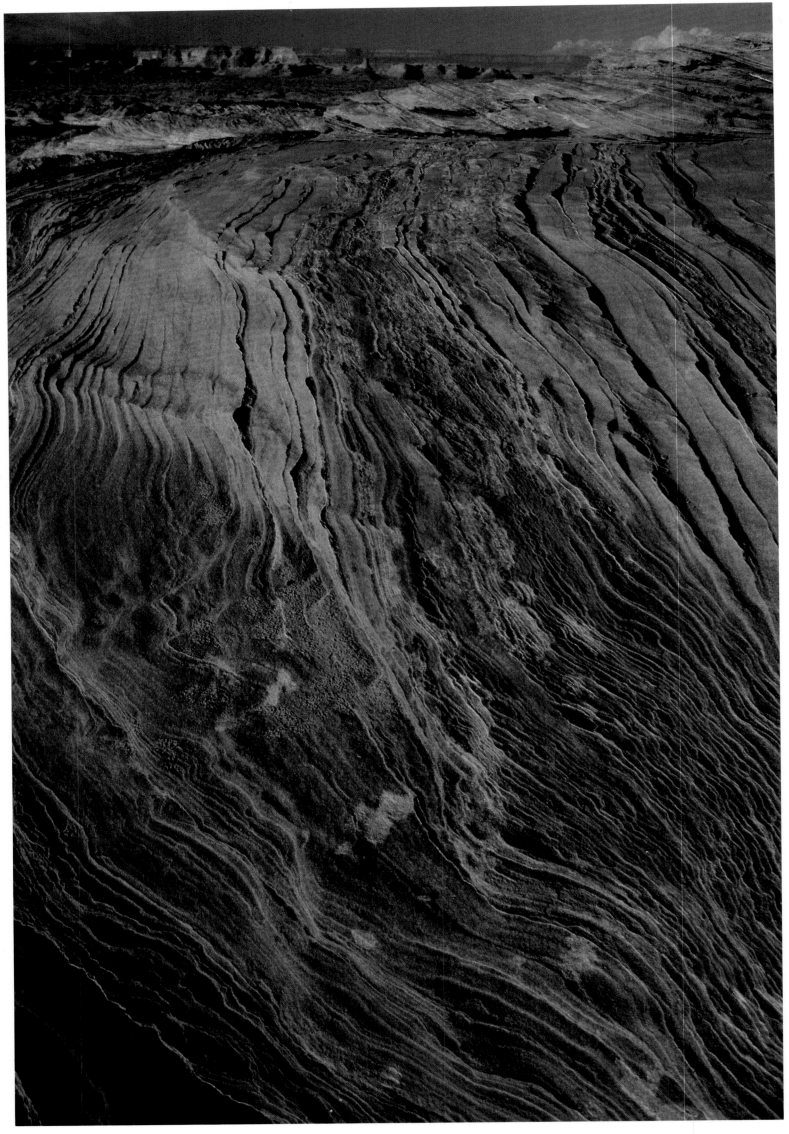

■ *Left:* The great stretches of Navajo Sandstone surrounding Lake Powell commemorate an era long ago when the region was an immense desert. ■ *Above:* Since its creation, Lake Powell has attracted more than two million visitors a year, who come to houseboat, fish, water-ski, swim, and explore the nearly one hundred side canyons that adjoin Glen Canyon.

GRAND CANYON

■ *Above:* Toroweap Point on the North Rim of the Grand Canyon drops straight down three thousand feet to the Colorado River. The river cuts through layers of rock deposited as many as 1.7 billion years ago. ■ *Right:* From Grandview Point on the South Rim, visitors can watch the canyon's changing moods and colors. ■ *Overleaf:* A lone wooden dory courses down the silt-laden Colorado, recalling the epic 1869 and 1871 river expeditions of explorer John Wesley Powell.

■ *Left:* A canyon wall throws a waxen reflection in Kanab Creek, one of the many minor tributaries of the Colorado along the lower Grand Canyon. ■ *Above:* Canyons within canyons deepen and widen through the constant cutting action of stream waters, which fade into a trickle during the early summer. ■ *Overleaf:* A float-trip down the Colorado offers the adventurous a unique perspective on canyon life. Since 1950, more than 250,000 people have made the journey.

■ *Above:* The elegant El Tovar Hotel was built on the South Rim of the Grand Canyon in 1905 to accommodate increasing numbers of visitors. In 1908, President Theodore Roosevelt designated the canyon a national monument, and in 1919 it became Grand Canyon National Park. Congress nearly doubled the size of the park in 1975. ■ *Right:* At Vasey's Paradise in Marble Canyon, water moving through porous sandstone reaches a layer of impenetrable rock and gushes out of the canyon wall.

■ *Left:* More than one hundred feet high, Deer Creek Falls is a popular stopping point for river-runners. ■ *Above:* Havasu Canyon with its travertine cascades has been called the Shangri-la of the Southwest. In the upper canyon the Havasupai Indians engage in small-scale farming. For over four thousand years, the Anasazi, Cohonina, and Cerbat Indians have intermittently made the Grand Canyon their home.

■ *Above:* Nearly a third of the total geologic history of the earth is dramatically recorded on the stratified rock walls of the Grand Canyon. ■ *Right:* Erosion does its work from above as well as below the canyon's rim. Along the North Rim, a weathered juniper holds on tenaciously through a raging thunderstorm — but only for a brief second in geologic time.

AFTERWORD

I've spent my life in wilderness: in the canoe country of Ontario, the Arctic, the Sierra, the Canadian Rockies. The canyons came late. In 1980, an assignment for National Geographic sent me to Zion and changed my life. Going to the canyons was going home. Deep home. Was I a lizard in a past life? A cougar? A cottonwood? It didn't matter. I was home again.

This book commemorates that homecoming and documents my discovery of the Canyon Country. Never have I had a more joyous assignment. There's magic in Canyon Country—magic and wonder and peace. Trying to capture those qualities on film was a challenge and delight.

Many times my experience went far beyond photography—times when, floating down a river or wandering across the slickrock, I traveled out beyond clock time, out of my human-centered world, to a place of fusion, to a sense of eternity. And from there, I could see a world where each person, each rock and tree and drop of water, played a part in the scheme of things—each part there to be cherished and celebrated.

Experiences like these restore my faith and rekindle in me a sense of wonder and a sense of hope. They could happen to me anywhere, but they happen most consistently in Canyon Country. They are part of the magic, and part of the reasons the canyons are so important to me. If my photographs communicate even a hint of that magic, then I will have succeeded in repaying a little of what the canyons have given me.

Books are not made just by those whose names appear on the jacket, and I wish to thank all those who helped me with CANYON COUNTRY: first, Kathy Stevens, for her understanding, companionship, and critical eye; second, Terri Martin, for introducing me to the canyons and teaching me their secrets; then Jane Walen, Mark and Stacy Austin, Linda Cordell, Marcus, Logan, and Pete Perry, Bob Jones, Bego, Vince Welch, Martin Litton, and Sue Halliday for serving as guides and teachers; Mickey Gallivan, Don Ware, Ann King, Harris and Love Advertising, and the Utah Travel Council for believing in my vision and making me a spokesman for Utah; finally, Taga-a-Long Tours, Grand Canyon Dories, Moab's Ramada Inn, Vernal's Dinosaur Inn, the Grand Old Ranch House, the San Juan Inn, the Bit n' Spur, TW Services, the Driftwood Lodge, Flanigan's, and the Under the Eaves Guest House for helping me along the way.

Dewitt Jones

I could not have written an essay with many voices without the generosity of Canyon Country's remarkable people who speak so eloquently here. I thank them—both those whose voices you hear in the finished text and those whose words do not appear: Pearl Baker, Green River, Utah; Steven Carothers and Steven Darden, Flagstaff, Arizona; Mary Craig, St. George, Utah; Clifford Duncan, Ft. Duchesne, Utah; Charles B. Hunt, Salt Lake City, Utah; Clifford Jake and Met Johnson, Cedar City, Utah; Michael Kabotie, Second Mesa, Arizona; Slim Mabery and Ken Sleight, Moab, Utah; Michael Marshall, Corrales, New Mexico; Herman Pollock, Tropic, Utah; Ed Smith, Oljato, Utah; John Stein, Albuquerque, New Mexico; Scott Truman, Castle Dale, Utah; and R. Gwinn Vivian, Tucson, Arizona.

I am grateful to the following people for helping me locate these voices: Robert Breunig, Chris Kincaid, Ken Mabery, Kathryn MacKay, Terri Martin, Tryntje Van Ness Seymour, David Stanley, Donald Trimble, and Terry Tempest Williams.

Kathy Stevens and Dewitt Jones kept me on the right track editorially. I thank them for their dedication. Lastly, I thank Dewitt Jones for suggesting that I speak for Canyon Country. It is an honor.

Stephen Trimble